WEST POINT

BATTLE HEROES

THE MEDAL OF HONOR

AN HISTORICAL SKETCHBOOK

Original pen and ink drawings by Robert A. Getz

Historical Narrative by Edward Merillat Moses

EDWARD M. MOSES AND ROBERT A. GETZ, PUBLISHERS
FAIRFAX STATION, VIRGINIA

Copyright © 1999 by Edward M. Moses and Robert A. Getz

Published by Edward M. Moses and Robert A. Getz, Publishers
PO Box 134, Fairfax Station, Virginia 22039

Cover Design by Robert A. Getz
Book Design by Edward M. Moses and Robert A. Getz, Publishers
Printed in the United States of America

Library of Congress Catalog Card Number 99 - 93273

ISBN 0-9648939-8-3

DEDICATION

This book is dedicated to the memory of

The Battle Heroes

of the

United States Military Academy

Recipients of

The Medal of Honor

To their parents, wives, sons and daughters, and the "Long Gray Line"
"May our country in the hour of need be ready for the foe."

*"That which thy fathers have bequeathed to thee
earn it anew if thou wouldst possess it."*

Goethe: *Faust*

ACKNOWLEDGEMENTS

I would like to acknowledge the following individuals and organizations for their valuable assistance and guidance in the development and completion of this book. First, I am indebted to my publishing partner Ed Moses, who did an outstanding job authoring the narrative while providing me with the latitude to work creatively. Second, I wish to thank my wife, Johnnie Lou, and my parents, Arthur and Lucille, for the motivation and support that each has given me. I would also like to acknowledge the help of my friends and associates at the Association of Graduates, the Special Collections Department of the West Point Library, and the Department of Foreign Languages at West Point. Their generous assistance helped me ensure that I brought the necessary accuracy to the creation of the many varied illustrations.

- Robert A. Getz
Illustrator

I wish to acknowledge certain individuals and organizations for their assistance in the creation of this book. First, I am indebted to my illustrator and publishing partner, Bob Getz, a staff member at the United States Military Academy, for his wonderful artwork and persistence. Once again, his original pen and ink sketches are creative, well researched, and pertinent. Second, I wish to acknowledge and thank my wife, Margaret Erskine Calhoun, for her numerous valuable suggestions and for the contribution of her editing skills.

At West Point, I want to thank Ms. Leslie Rose and the Association of Graduates, for her assistance in helping me to verify by computer the results of my search of the *Register of Graduates* for recipients of the Medal of Honor and the Distinguished Service Cross. Also at West Point, I want to thank my classmate, Mr. John Shelter, for providing me with library reference material that helped me to better understand historical detail relating to three of the Medal of Honor recipients. Ms. Suzanne Christhoff, who is with the Special Collections and Archives Departments of the U.S.M.A. Library, assisted Mr. Shelter in his efforts to obtain this information. I am also indebted to the staff of the U.S. Army Special Forces museum at Ft. Bragg, NC, and the staff of the museum located at Ft. Campbell, KY. Each provided a photograph of a Medal of Honor recipient we were unable to obtain elsewhere.

The staffs of both the Fairfax County and the City of Alexandria library systems in Virginia were very helpful in assisting in my acquisition of the historical detail necessary to support many of the Medal of Honor citations, particularly those relating to the *Indian Wars* and the *Spanish American War*. The staff of the U.S. Army Van Noy Library at Ft. Belvoir, Virginia, was extremely helpful in acquiring for my research several books from out-of-state libraries, including the Library of Congress. Of particular help at the Van Noy Library were Ms. Phyllis Cassler and Ms. Donna Landon, both of whom spent considerable time assisting me. They were both a great help in my acquisition of important history relating to the *Spanish American War* and the *Philippine Insurrection*.

- Edward M. Moses
Author

INTRODUCTION

Two of Webster's New World Dictionary definitions of the word *hero* are (1) "any person, especially a man, admired for qualities or achievements and regarded as an ideal or model" and (2) "the central figure in any important event or period, honored for outstanding qualities." Many of West Point's heroes who satisfy these two definitions can be found in our first collaborative book which is entitled *West Point, The Making of Leaders, An Historical Sketchbook*. That book included leaders in all of America's wars from the Mexican War to Desert Storm; the many graduate explorers, engineers, and railroad pioneers; the graduates who contributed to science, mathematics, mapping, education, politics, and sports; and our scientists and astronauts. For those who have not read this book, *The Making of Leaders* also had several chapters describing the Military Academy's current leadership and educational programs, and its physical and character development training.

Bob Getz and I would now like to introduce you to our newest historical sketchbook entitled *West Point Battle Heroes, The Medal of Honor, An Historical Sketchbook*. A third Webster Dictionary definition of a *hero* is "any person, especially a man, admired for courage, nobility, or exploits, especially in war." In the book you are now holding, you will find battle scenarios and award citations for eighty-two extraordinarily brave men who attended the Military Academy, and who received the Medal of Honor for heroism on the battlefield. In the nineteenth century the citations describing their heroic deeds are very brief, so it was necessary to add substantial historical detail from other sources so that you might better understand and more fully appreciate their acts of bravery. These men are West Point's *Battle Heroes*, the courageous recipients of America's highest decoration for valor, earned at the risk of their life while under enemy fire. Their heroic actions on the battlefield have bestowed honor on themselves, their families, their units, and the Military Academy.

When I was a boy I dreamed and read of battle heroes and their heroic deeds on battlefields. My boyhood heroes included Alexander the Great, Emperor Charlemagne, Roland, the Crusaders, William the Conqueror, Napoleon, Robert E. Lee, Thomas "Stonewall" Jackson, John "Blackjack" Pershing, and Douglas MacArthur. They were typical heroes of a young boy who wore cowboy "chaps", strapped on two holstered cap-pistols, and who prayed for the gift of a 1,000 shot Red Ryder BB gun at Christmas. Not surprisingly, these dreams and books helped influence me to enter the Military Academy at West Point, where I began an association with as fine a group of dedicated peers as one could ever hope to find. I'm sure that similar dreams and stories also led many of them to the Military Academy. While we then may have had those dreams in common as boys and young men, now we can all be proud of the mutual association that we share with the Military Academy and its eighty-two Medal of Honor recipients - West Point's revered *Battle Heroes*. These heroes have met the nation's highest and most exacting criteria for bravery. They have lived and died adhering to our honored West Point motto - *Duty, Honor, Country*. Each had in common with the others both the opportunity and the courage to perform wonderfully heroic deeds on the battlefield, as well as to set the highest battle standard for all of those who follow. They are our *Battle Heroes*.

I have included three appendices in this book that list medal awards to both graduates and former cadets. The first appendix lists the Medal of Honor recipient names by conflict, then by Association of Graduates number, and finally by class. The next two appendices list Military Academy recipients of the Distinguished Service Cross, the nation's second highest award for bravery. The second appendix lists recipients who received multiple awards of the Distinguished Service Cross, and the third lists recipients awarded a single Distinguished Service Cross. These two appendices are organized first by number of awards, then by Association of Graduates number, and finally by class.

Edward Merillat Moses
Class of 1954, U.S.M.A.

WEST POINT
BATTLE HEROES
THE MEDAL OF HONOR
AN HISTORICAL SKETCHBOOK

- TABLE OF CONTENTS -

MEDAL OF HONOR RECIPIENTS

(Posthumous awards are in Italics)

9

THE PYRAMID OF HONOR

The Medal of Honor (1862)

Distinguished Service Cross (1918) - Navy Cross (1919) - Air Force Cross (1960)

Defense Distinguished Service Medal (1970)
Distinguished Service Medal (1918)

Silver Star (1918)

Defense Superior Service Award (1976)
Legion of Merit (1942)
Distinguished Flying Cross (1926)
Soldier's Medal (1926) - Navy and Marine Corps Medal (1942) – Airman's Medal (1960)
Bronze Star (1942)
Meritorious Service Medal (1969)
Air Medal (1942)
Joint Service Commendation Medal [Army and Air Force (1963) - Navy (1967)]
Commendation Medal [Army (1945) - Navy (1944) - Air Force (1958)]

Purple Heart (1782)

The "bravest of the brave"

Adjacent to the Valley Forge National Historic Park in Pennsylvania is a "Grove of Trees" honoring America's greatest war heroes – the recipients of the Medal of Honor - our nation's highest award for valor. This "Grove of Trees" consists of fifty-two acres configured in the geographical shape of the United States of America. Each of the fifty states, Puerto Rico, and the District of Columbia occupies one of these acres, within which is erected a 7 foot 7 inch native stone obelisk placed on a 25 square foot brick patio foundation, similar in shape to the Washington Monument. On the several faces of each obelisk are mounted a donor plaque, the official seal of the state, and the inscribed name of every Medal of Honor recipient from that state. Each hero is further memorialized with a *living tree*, upon which is mounted a 4 x 6 inch steel plate bearing the medal recipient's name, rank, unit, and the date and location that the Medal of Honor was earned.

A quiet aura of history pervades the tranquility of this "Grove of Trees". Located on the grounds are a hillside band concert theater, a chapel, and a statue of General George Washington at prayer. The "Father of our Country" encamped his *Revolutionary War* army at nearby Valley Forge during the bitter winter of 1777-1778. Four years later he ordered the creation of the nation's first military decoration, the Purple Heart, which was to be awarded "for singular meritorious service", and which was first presented to three soldiers in 1783. Today, the Purple Heart is awarded for "wounds received while in combat with an armed enemy." The Medal of Honor and all of the other medals that are now awarded for bravery can be viewed along the "Patriots' Path" inside the "Grove of Trees". Together, these medals represent what is often referred to as the "Pyramid of Honor", America's awards for heroism arranged from top to bottom in their order of precedence. The Medal of Honor is at the top of the "Pyramid of Honor" and the Purple Heart is at its base. There are over 3,400 memorial trees in the "Grove of Trees", and each tree is a living testimonial to the bravery of the named American hero. Eighty-two memorial trees have been planted in memory of soldiers, airmen, and marines that attended the United States Military Academy at West Point.

11

In a little over two centuries, the United States of America has become the strongest and most prosperous nation in the world. Like most other great nations, wars have played a significant role in our nation's development and have contributed greatly to both our internal growth and our external expansion. The ancient philosopher Plato once said, "Only the dead have seen the end of war." Through war as an instrument of national policy, America has defended itself, expanded its borders, and achieved many national goals, while the nation's science and industry have been developed to a degree never before seen in the history of the world. However, while we have averaged seven wars in each of the past two centuries, for much of that time the selfless bravery of the soldiers, sailors, and marines that fought in those wars was not properly recognized. In fact, with the exception of the three *Revolutionary War* soldiers honored by General Washington in 1783 with the Purple Heart, almost a full century elapsed before **President Abraham Lincoln signed legislation on December 21, 1861, authorizing the nation's first medal for heroism - the Medal of Honor**. It was initially created for enlisted men of the Navy and Marine Corps, but six months later on July 12, 1862, Congress also authorized the Medal of Honor for Army enlisted men who **"shall most distinguish themselves by their gallantry in action and other soldier like qualities."** On March 3, 1863, this legislation was subsequently amended to include officers and was made retroactive to the start of the *Civil War*.

The first recipient of the Army Medal of Honor was a nineteen year old *Civil War* soldier named Jacob Parrott, one of six enlisted survivors of the April, 1862, clandestine "Mitchell Raid" into Georgia, popularly called the "Great Locomotive Chase". Ormsby M. Mitchell (Class of 1829), a senior staff officer with the Army of the Ohio, approved this secret mission to "take over a train, head north, and burn every bridge and trestle we cross." All twenty-one of the participating soldiers were captured and several were hung as spies. Parrott's group of six survivors had escaped after being initially captured, then were recaptured and later exchanged from a Confederate prisoner of war camp. The group were hastily summoned to Washington, D.C., to meet with the Secretary of War Edwin M. Stanton, who had decided to award each of the now nationally famous survivors with the recently approved Medal of Honor. Stanton selected Parrott, the youngest of the group, to receive the *first* Medal of Honor ever awarded and presented it to Parrott on March 25, 1863. The six honored survivors of the raid were then invited to the White House to visit with President Lincoln.

Following the *Civil War*, President Ulysses S. Grant (Class of 1843) personally presented the Medal of Honor twice in White House ceremonies, but the usual procedure at that time was to publish the recipient's name in either "Orders of the Day" or at troop formations. That practice soon gave way to mailing the medal to recipients by registered mail. On December 9, 1904, Major William E. Birkhimer (Class of 1870), a Medal of Honor recipient in the *Philippine Insurrection*, recommended that the Medal of Honor be presented "with formality and solemnity." On September 20, 1905, President Theodore Roosevelt signed an Executive Order directing that the award **"will always be made with formal and impressive ceremonies"**, and **"the recipient will, whenever practicable, be ordered to Washington, D.C., and the presentation will be made by the President, as Commander-in-Chief, or by such representative as the President may designate."**

On September 3, 1898, the U.S. War Department published General Orders No. 135, which established more demanding Medal of Honor criteria. Thenceforth, the medal would require **"distinguished bravery or conspicuous gallantry ... conduct that distinguishes a soldier above his comrades, and that involves risk of life, or the performance of more than ordinarily hazardous duty**." These orders further directed that the recommendation for the award must come from either the individual's immediate commanding officer, or the officer who either directly observed or had personal cognizance of the heroic act. A complete recital of the heroic deed was necessary, and the recommendation was to be accompanied by affidavits from all of the involved enlisted personnel, as well as the testimony of two eyewitnesses. Also, the individual's heroic act had to be supported by appropriate "after-action" or battle documentary reports.

Over half of all Medals of Honor were awarded for heroism during the *Civil War* and the *Indian Wars* from 1861 to 1898. Because of an inability to recognize different degrees of bravery, on June 3, 1916, Congress directed that an Army Board of five retired general officers be convened. Its purpose was to conduct a review of every Medal of Honor *previously awarded* and to determine the advisability of creating additional awards for bravery. On February 15, 1917, the Board purged from the official records the names of 910 of the 2,625 Medal of Honor recipients previously awarded. Congress accepted the Board's review and its records purge, and passed new legislation on July 9, 1918. It mandated new criteria for the Medal of Honor, and authorized the President **"to present, in the name of Congress, a Medal of Honor only to each person who while an officer or enlisted man of the Army, shall hereafter, in action involving actual conflict with an enemy, distinguish himself conspicuously by gallantry and intrepidity at risk of his life above and beyond the call of duty."** This *1918 Act* finally confirmed into law the three important Medal of Honor concepts of *"risk of ... life"*, *"gallantry"*, and *"actual conflict with an enemy"*.

Congress also accepted the Army Board's recommendation for additional medals and approved several new awards for bravery, including the Distinguished Service Cross (DSC), "to more fully single out and honor combat gallantry." Specifically, the President was **"authorized to present, but not in the name of Congress, a Distinguished Service Cross ... to any person who ... has distinguished ... or who shall hereafter distinguish himself or herself by extraordinary heroism in connection with military operations."** Recalling that in 1904 Congress had directed that all medal recommendations be submitted with official documents describing the details of the heroic act, the *1918 Act* added requirements that recommendations for all medal awards must be made by the individual's superior officer within two years, and that the medal must be presented to the recipient within three years. However, these time restrictions were later increased to three years and five years respectively. The *1918 Act* also established that the Medal of Honor was to be **"accorded supreme recognition"** over all other medals. Another award for heroism created by the *1918 Act*, in addition to the Distinguished Service Cross, was the Silver Star Citation. Importantly, however, the Medal of Honor was now firmly positioned at the top of the "Pyramid of Honor", and it was to be awarded only to the **"bravest of the brave!"**

On July 25, 1963, the Medal of Honor criteria were again modified to accommodate a dramatically changed world environment. This new and current criteria includes: **"for a deed of personal bravery or self-sacrifice above and beyond the call of duty only while the person is a member of the Armed Forces of the United States in action against an enemy of the United States, or while engaged in military operations involving conflict with an opposing foreign force, or while serving with friendly foreign forces engaged in armed conflict against an opposing armed force in which the United States is not a belligerent party."** Continually expanding Medal of Honor criteria have resulted in increasingly high standards that are best measured by higher posthumous award rates experienced by the medal recipients: 25% in World War I; 44% in World War II; 72% in Korea; and 65% in Vietnam. These statistics are clear proof that the Medal of Honor is awarded only at the **"risk of ... life, above and beyond the call of duty."**

The Medal of Honor Legion was organized in 1890 and quickly became a national organization. It was incorporated by the Congress in 1955 and is now known as the *Legion of Valor of the United States*. In 1916, Congress created the *Medal of Honor Roll* for recipients who were age 65 or older and provided them with a $10 monthly pension. This pension had been sponsored by the Legion for twenty-six years, in an attempt "to give the Medal of Honor the same position and rank among other military orders of the world which similar medals occupy". The size of the pension has been increased several times and is now $200 monthly. The pension age requirement was also changed several times, but was eliminated in 1965. On August 14, 1958, President Dwight David Eisenhower (Class of 1915) signed legislation that chartered the newly created *Congressional Medal of Honor Society of the United States*.

THE MEDAL OF HONOR

The appearance of the Medal of Honor has been modified several times by the military services. In 1904, Horace Porter (Class of 1860), the Ambassador to France, commissioned a jeweler in Paris to create several designs to be used in a selection process. Porter had received the Medal of Honor for his heroism at Chicamauga in the *Civil War*. The winning design in this process was patented on November 22, 1904, by General George L. Gillespie, Jr. (Class of 1862), in order to halt the rampant and abusive copying of the medal. In December, Gillespie, who also was a *Civil War* Medal of Honor recipient for his heroism at Bethesda Church in Virginia, permanently transferred his patent to "W.H. Taft and his successor or successors as Secretary of War of the United States of America." Following the expiration of that patent in 1918, congressional legislation was passed and signed on February 24, 1923, directing that any "imitation of the design of the medal was now forbidden by law." The final design of the *Army* Medal of Honor is officially described below:

> *"...made of silver, heavily electroplated in gold. The chief feature of the old medal, the five pointed star, has been retained, and in its center appears the head of Minerva, the highest symbol of wisdom and righteous war. Surrounding this central feature in circular form are the words 'United States of America' representing nationality. An open laurel wreath, enameled in green, encircles the star, and the oak leaves at the bases of the prongs of the star are likewise enameled in green to give prominence. The medal is suspended by a blue silk ribbon, spangled with 13 white stars representing the original States, and this ribbon is attached to an eagle supported upon a horizontal bar. Upon the bar, which is attached to two points of the star, appears the word 'Valor', indicative of the distinguished service represented by the medal. The reverse of the medal is plain so that the name of the recipient may be engraved thereon. On the reverse of the bar are stamped the words 'The Congress To ...'."*

CIVIL WAR

ROBERT A. GETZ 99©

There were no authorized medals for bravery when the *Civil War* began, but in late 1861 Congress created the Medal of Honor. It was the *only* authorized medal until just prior to World War I. The administrative selection of *Civil War* and *Indian War* medal recipients was a slow process that continued into the late 1890's. This long delay resulted in the substantial loss of most of the historical detail, and the early "citations" are not very descriptive and are quite brief. While unfortunate, this lack of historical detail does not detract from the credibility of the awards. Anyone familiar with the *Civil War* tactics of "dressed right" lines of attacking infantry, murderous grapeshot and canister fired from cannon at close range, and the resultant extraordinarily high casualty rates understands that *Civil War* soldiers were as brave as any that followed in our subsequent wars. However, little that has been written about these recipients has survived, and frequently the "citation" is but a single sentence. There were twenty-five *Civil War* Medal of Honor recipients who attended the United States Military Academy and who also fought in the Union Army. There were others who attended the Military Academy, equally brave, who fought for the Confederacy. They were friends, classmates, and former fellow officers who had served together while wearing the pre-war *Army Blue*. However, the Confederates received no medals for heroism, because none were authorized by the Confederacy.

On July 21, 1861, the first major battle of the *Civil War* was fought at Manassas Junction on high ground overlooking Bull Run Creek, twenty-seven miles west of Alexandria, Virginia. Both sides were inexperienced in the movement of brigade and larger sized formations, and they were closely matched in numbers. However, what was widely expected to be a joyful and victorious day for the Union Army, soon turned into a nightmarish headlong retreat. Union losses at Bull Run were about 4,500 out of a force of 37,000 men, including 1,500 taken prisoner. The Confederates lost about 2,000 men from a force that finally reached 40,000, as reinforcing units led by Joseph E. Johnston (Class of 1829) and Jubal Early (Class of 1837) arrived on the battlefield throughout the day. While the losses were nearly equal on both sides, the Union Army's morale was severely damaged. After the battle, newsman Horace Greeley wrote to President Lincoln, "If it is best for the country and for mankind that we make peace with the rebels at once and on their own terms, do not shrink even from that."

BENJAMIN

WILLCOX

TOMPKINS

AMES

Robert A. Getz '95 ©

16

BULL RUN AT MANASSAS JUNCTION

On May 24, 1861, General Irwin McDowell's (Class of 1838) Union army occupied the west bank of the Potomac River at Alexandria, Virginia. The "Army of the Potomac" had the mission of securing the western approaches to Washington from any Confederate threat. A week later, while on reconnaissance with 50 troopers near the City of Fairfax, **Charles H. Tompkins** (ex-cadet of the Class of 1851), a lieutenant with the 2nd U.S. Cavalry, encountered Confederate outposts. The *"quiet was broken only by a brisk dash into and through the village of Fairfax Court-House ... resulting in a loss of six on either side – and by an ambuscade at Vienna."* Tompkins' Medal of Honor citation states that he *"twice charged through the enemy's lines and, taking a carbine from an enlisted man, shot the enemy's captain."*

The first "Battle of Bull Run" at Manassas Junction began on July 21st, where **Orlando B. Willcox** (Class of 1847) commanded the 1st Michigan Infantry. His brigade was in the main attack force consisting of two divisions with the mission of turning the Confederate left flank. Initially this flanking maneuver succeeded, but then it failed as Confederate reinforcements began to arrive on the battlefield. Willcox was awarded the Medal of Honor for his *"most distinguished gallantry."* His citation states that he *"led repeated charges until wounded and taken prisoner."* Willcox was soon exchanged and later served as an acting corps commander at Fredericksburg and a division commander at Richmond. **Adelbert Ames** (Class of May, 1861) was a lieutenant assigned to Griffin's Battery of the 5th U.S. Artillery. He was with the main attack force attempting to turn the Confederate left flank. *"Griffin's Battery, which ... had done the most effective fighting throughout, was charged with effect by a Rebel regiment ... Three different attacks were repulsed with slaughter and the battery remained in our hands, though all its horses were killed."* Unsuccessful, however, the attacking Union Army was *"hurled back in utter rout and confusion"* and fled as rapidly as possible to re-cross Bull Run Creek. Ames' Medal of Honor citation states that he *"remained upon the field in command of a section of Griffin's Battery, directing its fire after being severely wounded and refusing to leave the field until too weak to sit upon the caisson where he had been placed by men of his command."* Ames later commanded a division in the "Army of the James River". **Samuel N. Benjamin** (Class of May, 1847) was a lieutenant with the 2nd U.S. Artillery at the "Battle of Bull Run". He was cited for his conduct at Bull Run Creek and in several subsequent engagements between July 1861 and May 1864, including the battles at Vicksburg and Spotsylvania. His Medal of Honor citation reads for *"Particularly distinguished service as an artillery officer."*

18

THE BATTLES AT HARPERS FERRY, SEVEN PINES, AND MALVERN HILL

Thomas "Stonewall" Jackson (Class of 1846) began a nearly flawless Virginia "Shenandoah Valley Campaign" with a surprise attack on the Federal forces at Front Royal and Winchester. Routed and panic-stricken, the Union Army fled across the Potomac River into Maryland at the city of Williamsport on May 26, 1862. Jackson quickly moved toward the strategically important Federal arsenal at Harpers Ferry, located at the convergence of the Potomac and Shenandoah Rivers. Alarmed at this threatened invasion of Maryland, a substantial Federal force was diverted to the Shenandoah Valley from eastern Virginia in an attempt to encircle and trap Jackson. **Rufus Saxton** (Class of 1849), a brigadier general, successfully defended Harpers Ferry with 7,000 severely demoralized troops from May 26th to May 30th. The town was not taken, and Jackson, who quietly withdrew down the Valley, did not invade Maryland. Saxton's Medal of Honor citation notes that he displayed *"distinguished gallantry and good conduct in the defense."*

Meanwhile in eastern Virginia, George B. McClellan (Class of 1846) began his "Peninsular Campaign", which he envisioned as a turning movement followed by a rapid advance on Richmond from a newly established base of operations at Fort Monroe, Virginia. After repositioning his army by ship, McClellan advanced slowly up the peninsula to Fair Oaks Station, seven miles from Richmond and mid-way between the James and Chickahominy Rivers. On June 1, 1862, the Confederate commander Joseph E. Johnston (Class of 1829) attacked him at Fair Oaks Station. **Oliver O. Howard** (Class of 1854), a brigade commander, received the Medal of Honor for heroism in the "Battle of Seven Pines" at Fair Oaks Station - a battle that cost him his right arm. His citation states that he *"led the 61st New York Infantry in a charge in which he was twice severely wounded in the right arm, necessitating its amputation."* Nicknamed "The Bible General", Howard's "reputation among Negroes was higher than that of any other white man in the country." Later, he became a corps commander, and in 1881 he was appointed Superintendent of the Military Academy. O. O. Howard also founded Howard University in Washington, D.C.; organized an integrated Congregational Church; and was director of a bank for Negroes.

1st Lieutenant **John M. Wilson** (Class of 1860) was awarded the Medal of Honor for heroism on August 6, 1862, at the battle for Malvern Hill, as McClellan withdrew down the peninsula on orders from a discouraged President Lincoln. Robert E. Lee (Class of 1829) was in command of the newly renamed "Army of Northern Virginia". Wilson's citation states that *"he remained on duty, while suffering from an acute illness and very weak, and participated in the action of that date. A few days previous he had been transferred to a staff corps, but preferred to remain until the close of the campaign, taking part in several actions."* An engineer officer, Wilson later completed the construction of the Washington Monument in 1888-1889. He was appointed Superintendent of the Military Academy in 1889, where he authorized the very first Army-Navy football game played on November 29, 1890. Wilson was appointed Chief of Engineers in 1897 and was elected President of the Association of Graduates in 1911.

GREENE

HATCH

Robert A. Getz '90

ANTIETAM CREEK AT SHARPSBURG

Having successfully blocked McClellan's "Peninsular Campaign", Lee made the daring strategic decision to carry the war into the North. Moving quickly, while J.E.B. Stuart's (Class of 1854) cavalry screened the right flank of the "Army of Northern Virginia", he crossed the Potomac River into Maryland, seizing Frederick on September 6, 1862, and Hagerstown four days later. Lee positioned his army east and north of Sharpsburg, while a typically cautious McClellan, who fortuitously had a captured copy of Lee's operational plans in his hands, still delayed four days before finally ordering a rapid march to the northwest to meet Lee's invasion threat. His leading corps, commanded by Joseph Hooker (Class of 1837), came upon D. H. Hill's (Class of 1842) Confederate division occupying a blocking position at Turner's Gap on South Mountain, east of Sharpsburg. It was there that **John P. Hatch** (Class of 1845), who commanded the 1st Division of Hooker's leading corps, won *"a hard-fought engagement at South Mountain in which the Federals, led by Hatch and Doubleday, were victorious."* Abner Doubleday (Class of 1842), one of Hatch's brigade commanders, "devised and named the game of baseball at Cooperstown, New York." The battle at Turner's Gap was *"violent and protracted."* Hatch's troops were later commended for their great *"courage and determination"* while outnumbered and low on ammunition. Hatch's Medal of Honor citation states that on September 14th, he *"was severely wounded while leading one of his brigades in the attack under heavy fire from the enemy."*

Both armies were now concentrated near Sharpsburg, with Antietam Creek separating the two southern flanks of each. The battle began north of Sharpsburg at dawn on September 17th, with three successive corps sized assaults on the Confederate left flank. Meanwhile on the Confederate right, Ambrose Burnside (Class of 1847) moved forward slowly to attack the Confederate southern, right flank. He crossed Antietam Creek near noon, and in the middle of the afternoon he finally began a coordinated frontal attack that was quickly repulsed by Confederate reinforcements. It was against Burnside's force that D.H. Hill's division defended from a sunken road that came to be called the "Bloody Lane". The battle fought at Antietam Creek was ferocious. It produced *"the war's single bloodiest day,"* and it was *"the bloodiest battle ever fought on American soil."* A total of between 22,500 and 26,500 soldiers from both sides became casualties on that day. **Oliver D. Greene** (Class of 1854), an artillery brigadier general, received the Medal of Honor for his heroism at Sharpsburg on September 17th. Greene's citation reads simply that he *"formed the columns under heavy fire."*

PORTER

SCHOFIELD

CARR

BOURKE

ROBERT A. GETZ 99©

22

WILSON'S CREEK, ELKHORN TAVERN, STONE'S RIVER, AND CHICAMAUGA

Missouri's lead mines were an important strategic natural resource. The *Civil War* came to Missouri for the first time in June of 1861. On August 10th, a hard battle was fought ten miles south of Springfield at Wilson's Creek, where the Federal's Nathaniel Lyon (Class of 1841) attacked a superior force. Lyon was initially successful, but was wounded twice and his horse was killed. Badly dazed, *"he walked a few paces to the rear, saying to his Adjutant John Schofield, 'I fear the day is lost.' Schofield replied, 'No General; let us try them once more."* **John M. Schofield** (Class of 1853) then led a regimental charge that earned him the Medal of Honor. His citation states that he *"was conspicuously gallant in leading a regiment in a successful charge against the enemy."* Colonel Plummer of the 11th Missouri Infantry said: *"Maj. Schofield stated to me ... it was a perfect rout - that the enemy fled in the wildest confusion. He said ... the enemy ... dead were piled up so thick that he could not ride over them, but had to make a considerable detour."* Schofield was Superintendent at West Point in 1876 and was elected President of the Association of Graduates in 1900.

In early 1862 the Union Army pushed through Missouri. They entered the mountains of northwest Arkansas and took up positions on Pea Ridge. On March 6th and 7th they were attacked by a very large combined force consisting of Confederates and Indians. Colonel **Eugene A. Carr** (Class of 1850) commanded the 3rd Illinois Cavalry at the ensuing Pea Ridge battle of Elkhorn Tavern. He was wounded three times and was awarded the Medal of Honor for his heroism. Carr's citation states that he *"directed the deployment of his command and held his ground, under a brisk fire of shot and shell in which he was several times wounded."* Carr later won fame as a renowned Indian fighter and was given the name "War Eagle" by the western tribes.

On December 31, 1862, **John G. Bourke** (Class of 1869) was serving as a cavalry private at Stone's River in Tennessee. Of interest, the Confederates under Braxton Bragg (Class of 1837) and the Union Army under William S. Rosecrans (Class of 1842) coincidentally had identical battle plans at Stone's River - to attack the other's right flank. Rosecrans massed his troops left, but his right flank suddenly *"was shattered to fragments"* by Bragg's force and was driven off. The Confederates were finally stopped by the *"almost unparalleled heroism of the division of General William B. Hazen"* (Class of 1855). Bourke was in Hazen's division. His Medal of Honor citation reads for *"gallantry in action."* After the war, he entered and graduated from the Military Academy. Following graduation, Bourke spent many years fighting Indians, and in 1886 he was serving with George Crook (Class of 1852) at Geronimo's surrender.

By June 1863, Rosecrans had driven Bragg out of Tennessee and into Georgia. Reinforced, Bragg counterattacked at Chicamauga Creek on September 19-20, breaking through the Federal lines. George H. Thomas (Class of 1840) *"with a desperate firmness hardly equaled in the annals of war, held the left flank until nightfall."* Captain **Horace Porter** (Class of 1860) was with Thomas at Chicamauga and earned his Medal of Honor on the 20th of June. Porter's citation states that he *"While acting as a volunteer aide, at a crucial moment when the lines were broken, rallied enough fugitives to hold the ground under heavy fire long enough to effect the escape of wagon trains and batteries."* In 1897 Porter was appointed Ambassador to France, and in 1906 he was elected President of the Association of Graduates. Porter is credited with locating and recovering the long lost remains of America's naval hero John Paul Jones, which he delivered to the U.S. Naval Academy for interment. For this singular act, Porter received the "Thanks of Congress" in 1906.

THE BATTLES AT FREDERICKSBURG AND GETTYSBURG

After the "Battle of Antietam" at Sharpsburg, Ambrose Burnside (Class of 1847) assumed command of the Union Army. In early December of 1862, the two opposing armies met again at Fredericksburg on the banks of the Rappahannock River. Burnside crossed the river on the 12th of December and attacked the next day. Six ranks of Confederate infantry stood in a sunken road on Mayre's Heights, firing from behind a protective stone wall. Ten thousand Federals fell in front of that wall, and not one came closer than 100 feet. While watching from high ground, General Lee said, *"It is well that war is so terrible; men would love it too much."* A Federal newspaper printed, *"It can hardly be in human nature for men to show more valor, or generals to manifest less judgement."* Colonel **Zenas R. Bliss** (Class of 1854) led the attack on Mayre's Heights and was awarded the Medal of Honor for his bravery. His citation reads: *"This officer, to encourage his regiment which had never before been in action, and which had been ordered to lie down to protect itself from the enemy's fire, arose to his feet, advanced in front of the line, and himself fired several shots at the enemy at short range, being fully exposed to their fire at the time."* Lee won the battle at Fredericksburg and five months later he was victorious again at Chancellorsville. Following the battle at Chancellorsville, Lee made his fateful decision to turn the "Army of Northern Virginia" north toward Pennsylvania, where he would come to a small town named Gettysburg.

Alexander S. Webb (Class of 1855) led a brigade of Pennsylvania regiments in John Gibbon's (Class of 1847) division at Gettysburg in July of 1863. On the third day of fighting, Webb's brigade was deployed on Cemetery Ridge around a *"little clump of trees"*, which was to be the centerpoint of George Pickett's (Class of 1846) disasterous and bloody Confederate charge on July 3rd. Gibbon observed that the ridge was *"the most infernal pandemonium it has ever been my fortune to look upon."* He said, *"the smoke hung a couple of feet off the ground ... only the legs of the gunners were visible."* Two of Webb's regiments were behind a low stone wall and fence, while two others were behind the ridge in the rear in reserve. When the cannonade smoke lifted, these *"old soldiers"* looked west toward Seminary Ridge and saw a sight that they were never to forget. *"There it was ... the grand pageantry ... beautiful and majestic and terrible: fighting men lined up for a mile and a half from flank to flank, slashed red flags overhead, soldiers marching elbow to elbow, officers with drawn swords, sunlight gleaming from thousands of musket barrels, lines dressed as if on parade. Up and down the Federal firing line ran a murmur: 'There they are ... There comes the infantry.'"* Pickett's men attacked through *"a ghastly debris of guns, knapsacks, blanket rolls, severed human heads, and arms and legs and parts of bodies tossed into the air by the impact of shot."* Webb was wounded. Pickett's division surged onward and *"a moan went up from the field, distinctly to be heard amid the roar of the battle."* A penetrated regiment withdrew toward the crest, but reinforcements quickly arrived, and they helped Webb complete the final destruction of Pickett's division. Webb received the Medal of Honor for his bravery on Cemetery Ridge. His citation reads that he displayed *"Distinguished personal gallantry in leading his men forward at a critical period in the contest."* After the war, Webb became President of the College of the City of New York, where he served for 33 years.

SPOTSYLVANIA, DAVENPORT BRIDGE, AND OLD COLD HARBOR

In March of 1864, Ulysses S. Grant (Class of 1843) assumed overall command of the Federal forces. Lincoln's orders were to "go after Lee." Grant's first major contact with Lee was at the "Battle of the Wilderness", won by Lee when he turned both Federal flanks. After that battle both armies continued maneuvering to the southeast, as Grant attempted to threaten Richmond. Finally, Lee dug in at Spotsylvania Court House, where the lead Federal division under **John C. Robinson** (ex-cadet of the Class of 1839) found him on May 8th, following a rapid night march. Robinson had no opportunity to concentrate his division, but was ordered to attack immediately. He was well known as *"one of the Army of the Potomac's bravest and most distinguished division commanders."* The attack failed, but his *"most distinguished gallantry"* earned him the Medal of Honor. His citation reads that he *"placed himself at the head of the leading brigade in a charge upon the enemy's breastworks; was severely wounded."* Robinson's wound cost him his left leg and removal from field duty. On May 10th, cavalry under Philip H. Sheridan (Class of 1853) were attacked crossing the North Anna River. **Abraham Arnold** (Class of 1858) had the mission of securing the Davenport Bridge with his 5th U.S. Cavalry and protecting Sheridan's flank as he crossed at a ford east of the bridge. Unexpectedly, Confederate cavalry crossed at *"hidden fords"* and cut off Arnold's cavalry. *"In withdrawing, this gallant regiment, with its accomplished commander, Captain Arnold, at its head, charged and made its way through a superior force of the enemy which, by crossing blind fords on the river, had interposed between him and the main command."* Arnold's citation states that he *"by a gallant charge against a superior force of the enemy, extricated his command from a perilous position in which it had been ordered."*

Meanwhile, Grant again decided to sidestep to the southeast, once more flanking Lee while continuing to threaten Richmond. It was strategically important that the critical road junction of Old Cold Harbor be seized quickly. 1st Lieutenant **George L. Gillespie, Jr.** (Class of 1862), an engineer officer assigned to Grant's headquarters at Bethesda Church on May 31st, was asked to carry an important message to Sheridan, Grant's cavalry commander. Passing through the Confederate lines, he was twice captured and escaped both times. Gillespie's Medal of Honor citation states that he *"exposed himself to great danger by voluntarily making his way through the enemy's lines to communicate with Gen. Sheridan. While rendering this service he was captured, but escaped; again came in contact with the enemy, was again ordered to surrender, but escaped by dashing away under fire."* The battle at Old Cold Harbor began late on June 1st with an attack by two Federal divisions. **Guy V. Henry** (Class of May, 1861), a brigade commander, received the Medal of Honor for his heroism on that day. *"Under a severe fire they crossed the open field ... and carried the rifle pits, capturing about 250 prisoners."* Henry's citation states that he *"led the assaults of his brigade upon the enemy's works, where he had 2 horses shot under him."* A final grand attack on June 3rd was the *"bloodiest charge of the war, bloodier even than Pickett's charge at Gettysburg."* In only eight minutes at Old Cold Harbor, eight thousand Federals fell to Lee's *"interlocking fields of fire"*. In 1876, Henry was with General George Crook (Class of 1852) at the headwaters of the Rosebud where he was severely wounded, losing half his face fighting the Sioux Indians.

STANLEY

BAIRD

BEEBE

BEAUMONT

28

MONETTE'S FERRY, FRANKLIN, JONESBORO, AND WEST HARPETH RIVER

In 1864, William T. Sherman (Class of 1840) began to systematically annihilate the Confederate western armies and their war production base. In Louisiana, the "Red River Campaign" to capture Shreveport began in early March. The Federals, supported by gunboats moving up the Red River, captured Ft. de Russy and Alexandria. After leaving the river and the protection of the gunboats, the advance guard was suddenly surprised and routed at Mansfield on April 8th. As the Federal force retreated to Alexandria, pursuing Confederates attacked the main body at Pleasant Hill and inflicted heavy losses of 3,000 men, capturing twenty artillery pieces and the entire supply train. 1st Lieutenant **William S. Beebe** (Class of 1863) was awarded the Medal of Honor on April 23rd for bravery at Monette's Ferry on the Cane River, where the Union Army had to force a river crossing against a strong Confederate force. His citation states that he "*voluntarily led a successful assault on a fortified position.*" The Federal commander was later relieved, and "the Red River expedition was a source of much shame and mortification to the national government." On August 31st in Georgia, the final battle for Atlanta was fought at Jonesboro, where John B. Hood (Class of 1853) desperately attacked the Federal right flank in order to prevent his complete envelopment. His attack failed and he began the evacuation of Atlanta the next day. **Absalom Baird** (Class of 1849), a division commander, participated in the battle at Jonesboro and was awarded the Medal of Honor for heroism, when he "*voluntarily led a detached brigade in an assault upon the enemy's works.*" Baird later became the Army Inspector General in 1885.

Hood escaped by a circuitous route northwest into Tennessee, where he encountered John Schofield's corps at Franklin on November 30th of 1864. He attacked in mid-afternoon with 20,000 men, routing two forward-deployed Federal brigades and pursuing them into their breastworks. The Union Army counterattacked, and hand-to-hand fighting continued until dark. In this "*grand assault,*" the Confederates lost 6,000 men and twelve of their general officers. **David S. Stanley** (Class of 1852) was wounded and cited for bravery at Franklin. His citation states that he "*at a critical moment, rode to the front of one of his brigades, reestablished its lines, and gallantly led it in a successful assault.*" In 1893 Stanley became Governor of the Soldiers Home in Washington, D.C., and then President of the Association of Graduates in 1898. Schofield withdrew from Franklin to Nashville where he joined up with General Thomas. Together they attacked and overwhelmed Hood's left flank on December 15th. The battles at Franklin and Nashville completed "the virtual destruction of John B. Hood's 'Army of Tennessee'." Thomas aggressively pursued Hood, who organized a strong defensive position one-mile north of the West Harpeth River. In the twilight of December 17th, the 4th U.S. Cavalry rode over and through the center of his defense and its supporting batteries. **Eugene B. Beaumont** (Class of May, 1861) was aide-de-camp to James H. Wilson (Class of 1860), the commander of the Federal cavalry corps. For his bravery at West Harpeth River and later at Selma, Alabama, he was awarded the Medal of Honor. Beaumont's citation reads that he "*obtained permission from the corps commander to advance upon the enemy's position with the 4th U.S. Cavalry, of which he was a lieutenant; led an attack upon a battery, dispersed the enemy, and captured the guns. At Selma, Alabama, charged at the head of his regiment into the second and last line of the enemy's works.*"

BENTAVNE DU PONT

THE BATTLES OF CEDAR CREEK AND FIVE FORKS

The "Shenandoah Valley Campaign" of 1864 pitted Sheridan against Jubal A. Early (Class of 1837) for control of the southern "bread basket". On October 19th, a decisive battle was fought at Cedar Creek, where Early turned and counterattacked pursuing Federals. Sheridan happened to be visiting friends in Winchester, when *"Early cautiously approached the Union camp, surprised it, burst in, carried the position, captured the artillery and sent the routed troops flying in confusion toward Winchester."* Sheridan encountered his fleeing troops while returning from his visit to Winchester, rallied them, and turned the apparent defeat into *"one of the greatest tactical and strategic victories of the war,"* thus ending all future strife in the Shenandoah Valley. **Henry A. DuPont** (Class of May, 1861), a captain with the 5th U.S. Artillery, was at Cedar Creek and received the Medal of Honor for his heroism there. His citation reads: *"By his distinguished gallantry, and voluntary exposure to the enemy's fire at a critical moment when the Union line had been broken, encouraged his men to stand up to their guns, checked the advance of the enemy, and brought off most of his pieces."* In 1875, DuPont left the army and joined his father, Henry DuPont (Class of 1833), in the Delaware family powder mill business that was destined to become the world's largest chemical company.

Grant finally tired of trying to overcome the well-built field fortifications that Lee was so adept at building and was using to great advantage. He decided that the only thing *"that would pull Lee out of the trenches to fight"* was to threaten the Confederate supply lines by seizing the strategic road center at Five Forks. On April 1st, 1865, *"a severe battle was fought at Five Forks on the Southside Railroad."* The Confederate commander, George Pickett, happened to be enjoying a clambake some miles away when Romeyn B. Ayres' (Class of 1847) Federal division attacked his left flank. Ayres' skirmish line moved through a thickly wooded area and then advanced across an open field that sloped down toward dense woods. A heavy fire came from the edge of the woods and *"the skirmish line halted and seemed to waver."* A Confederate observer said *"the Federal line staggered a little,"* recovered, *"and executed the movement to the left in good order."* 1st Lieutenant **William H. H. Benyaurd** (Class of 1863), a bridging operations engineer officer, was there with the skirmishers and was awarded the Medal of Honor for his heroism. The citation states that Benyaurd *"with one companion, voluntarily advanced in a reconnaissance beyond the skirmishers where he was exposed to imminent peril; also, in the same battle, rode to the front with the commanding general to encourage wavering troops to resume the advance, which they did successfully."* The Confederate force was defeated and Sheridan's aggressive pursuit captured 6,000 prisoners. Grant's strategy had been proven correct. Lee abandoned his positions at Petersburg, Virginia, and withdrew toward the western Virginia mountains with Sheridan in hot pursuit. A few days later, Lee surrendered to Grant at Appomattox Court House on April 9th of 1865.

CIVIL WAR HUMOR

In spite of the terrible bloodletting of the *Civil War*, there were many occasions when soldiers from both sides engaged in levity and were friendly with one another, even to the extent of sharing water, food and tobacco. A sense of humor was important to help maintain their sanity in a world that must have frequently seemed out of control. One such instance occurred near the Tennessee - Georgia border, when an Ohio infantryman created new words for *The Charge of the Light Brigade*. His inspiration for these new lyrics came when a poorly picketed line of Federal mules panicked from the noise and flashing lights of a nearby heavy night engagement. Breaking free, the mules wildly charged into the Confederate lines where they were mistaken for a Federal cavalry charge. The Ohio infantryman memorialized this truly hysterical occasion by writing:

> *"Half a mile, half a mile*
> > *Half a mile onward,*
> *Right toward the Georgia troops*
> > *Broke the two hundred.*
> *'Forward, the Mule Brigade;*
> > *Charge for the rebs!' they neighed.*
> *Straight for the Georgia troops,*
> > *Broke the two hundred.*
>
> *When can their glory fade?*
> > *O The wild charge they made!*
> *All the world wondered.*
> > *Honor the charge they made;*
> *Honor the Mule Brigade,*
> > *Long-eared two hundred."*

As in all wars, letters from pen pals, girlfriends, sweethearts and family were greatly anticipated. *In-Search-Of* advertisements in newspapers were not Twentieth Century ideas. On March 6, 1864, the *Chattanooga Gazette* printed the following plaintive request of a Federal trooper:

> *"Any young lady not sufficiently homely to frighten a dog out of a butcher*
> *shop nor sufficiently beautiful to bewitch the idle shoulder straps* [officers]
> *about town can get up considerable fun by commencing a correspondence*
> *with Aaron, Chattanooga Post Office."*

And was there ever an army that didn't complain about the food? A soldier trying to chew a piece of beef complained facetiously that the meat was carved from a bull that was *"too old for the conscript law."* Another asked, *"Boys, I was eating a piece of hardtack this morning, and I bit on something soft; what do you think it was?"* His companion replied, *"A worm?"*. The answer: *"No, by God, it was a ten penny nail."*

Even speech dialects were a source of Civil War amusement:

> *"Don't that beat all. Those rebels came all the way up here to fight over rodents."*
> *"Rodents! What do you mean."*, answered his companion.
> *"Well, they said the reason they was up here fightin' was because we're trying*
> *to take away their 'rats'* [rights].*"*

THE INDIAN WARS

Robert A. Getz 99 ©

In March of 1890, after nearly a century of bloody frontier fighting the United States Senate finally voted that we were at war with the Indians! The fighting officially ended eight years later at the "Battle of Wounded Knee", concluding "nineteen fairly well-defined wars against the Indians." As settlers migrated west, aided by the new transcontinental railroads, buffalo herds were destroyed and "treaty guaranteed" Indian lands were steadily encroached upon. The many problems arising from broken promises were further exacerbated by the conduct of righteous "do-gooders" who portrayed the Indian as the "noble red man", and "carpetbaggers" who sold whiskey and repeating rifles to frustrated Indians. Bitter fighting marked the second half of the nineteenth century as Indians fled from rampant despair on reservations that were too frequently mismanaged by corrupt agents of the Indian Bureau. General Philip Sheridan (Class of 1853) summarized the chaos best when he wrote, "There are too many fingers in the pie, ... too much money to be made; and it is in the interest of the nation and of humanity to put an end to this inhuman farce."

Twenty-one of the Medals of Honor awarded in the *Indian Wars* went to officers who began their military careers attending West Point. Most of these medal awards were associated with campaigns against the Nez Perces led by Chief Joseph in Idaho, Wyoming and Montana; the Chihenne Apaches led by Victorio and Nana in New Mexico, Arizona and Texas; Geronimo's Chiricahua Apaches in Arizona and Mexico; Natiotish's White Mountain Apaches in Arizona; and Big Foot's Miniconjous Sioux in the Dakotas. The Northern Plains tribes included the Sioux, Pawnee, Crow, Shoshone, Northern Cheyenne, Arapahoe, Blackfeet, and Assiniboine tribes. The Southern Plains tribes were the Comanche, Kiowa, Apache, Southern Cheyenne, and Arapahoe tribes. Unlike the *Civil War*, the opposing forces were typically quite small. One of the larger tribes, "The Seven Tribes of Teton Sioux", numbered only 16,000, of which 4,000 were warriors. There were also "The Five Civilized Tribes", which included the Cherokee, Creek, Choctaw, Chicasaw and Seminole tribes. In order to protect the many dispersed settlements along a plains frontier that was many miles in length, the army was only able to deploy several thousand troops, mostly cavalry, that were posted in a loose system of mutually supporting forts.

33

LIFE ON THE FRONTIER

The Plains Indian belonged to the Ganowanian, or Bow-and-Arrow, family of men. They lived for the chase, and they survived in the woodlands with the wild animals and had unlimited hunting grounds. Their paradise was the forest, the hills, and the rivers, and the tribe was their family. They had both national and tribal councils for the purpose of debating policy and making decisions. Unlike the European family, where kinship lines diverged based on the male line of descent, the Indian tribe's line of descent was established by the female line and converged on the granddaughter. Thus, all uncles were recognized as fathers and all aunts as mothers. Cousins were sisters and brothers; nieces were daughters; and nephews were sons. The two key leaders of every tribe were the Chieftain, or "Sachem", and the Medicine Man. The Chieftain's "authority and right of command extended no further than to be foremost in danger, most cunning in savage strategy, bravest in battle." The Medicine Man was a self-appointed physician and prophet. His influence "depended upon himself and the voluntary respect of the nation." Indians believed in a *Great Spirit* and were very superstitious, but they had no temples. There were both good spirits and bad spirits. The Indian had a great "passion for war" as a primary means to redress grievances. He pursued offenders with "a personal, vindictive, and bloody vengeance." Revenge was both a noble pursuit and a virtue. In order to achieve it, he used surprise, ambush and massacre. His weapon of choice was the bow and arrow, a weapon with a deadly accuracy at a range of more than 200 yards. His mobility was provided by the horse, reintroduced by the Spaniards after having been lost for 7,000 years. It was a horse culture, and they were great horsemen - perhaps the finest light cavalry ever.

Twenty-one men held the position of Commissioner of the Bureau of Indian Affairs from 1834 to 1890. Almost all were "political hacks", and they personally pocketed an estimated 85% of all congressional appropriations for Indian subsistence, education, and land payments. By 1880, there were 187 Indian reservations holding 243,000 Indians governed by 2,500 officials, "the overwhelming majority of whom were incompetent, corrupt or a combination of the two." A stated intent of the "reservation system" was to undermine and destroy the tribal organization and to replace Indian tribal customs. At the San Carlos Reservation in Arizona, Bureau Inspectors found agents selling Indian goods on the open market, diverting cattle to their own private herds, and feeding their personal cattle on government supplied grain. A congressman observed that "No branch of the national government is so spotted with fraud, so tainted with corruption, so utterly unworthy of a free and enlightened government, as this Indian Bureau."

Soldiering on the frontier was not a "bed of roses". The Army posts were widely scattered and units were usually severely under strength, a result of the post-*Civil War* reductions in the army. The pay was low, and promotions through the field grade ranks were based on a regimental system that was incredibly slow. However, army life was a career that provided camaraderie not found elsewhere; and for adventurous souls, life on the frontier had its exciting moments. Frederick E. Phelps (Class of 1870) said on reporting to Ft. Bayard, New Mexico: "The locality was all that could be desired; the Post everything undesirable ... a flat dirt roof ... that in the summer brought down rivulets of liquid mud: in winter the hiding place of the tarantula and the centipede ... Six hundred miles from the railroad ... with nothing to eat but government rations ... ." As late as 1884, soldiers on duty in the west quipped that if they wanted to be well cared for, they must transfer to either a military prison or a cemetery. Most posts encouraged vegetable gardens. An officer whose garden was destroyed by locusts in 1873, remarked that "The damn hoppers came along, by God, and ate my garden, by God, then the birds ate the hoppers, by God, and we killed and ate the birds, by God, so that we were even in the long run, by God." Anson Mills, who attended the Military Academy with the class of 1860, remarked as his steam boat cast off from Fort Yuma: "We took off our shoes and beat out the dust of Arizona over the rail, at the same time cursing the land." Most looked back on their frontier duty as tough but happy years that were replete with bonding and excitement.

CARTER

THE KIOWAS AND COMANCHES RAID TEXAS

In August 1870 a Texas newspaper wrote that, "the counties of Llano, Mason, and Gillespie swarm with savages. The farmers are shot down in their fields, and their stock is stolen before their eyes ... Not for twenty years back have the Indians been so bold, well armed and numerous as now. At Llano the frontier is breaking up." The Kiowa and the Comanche tribes had left the Ft. Sill and Ft. Darlington Reservations in Oklahoma and were raiding throughout west-central Texas. At Ft. Richardson on the Trinity River, east of the Brazos River, Ranald S. MacKenzie (Class of 1862) *"commanded the 4th Cavalry with a diligence and discipline that made it the best of all cavalry regiments."* The 4th U.S. Cavalry's area of operations included from the Brazos River to the northeast beyond the Red River, and then to the Oklahoma reservation sanctuaries near Ft. Sill. On October 10, 1871, **Robert G. Carter** (Class of 1870), a 2nd lieutenant with the 4th Cavalry, earned the *first* Medal of Honor awarded a West Pointer for heroism in the Indian Wars. The action occurred at the Brazos River against a superior Indian force. Carter's citation states that he "*held the left of the line with a few men during the charge of a large body of Indians, after the right of the line had retreated, and by delivering a rapid fire succeeded in checking the enemy until the other troops came to the rescue.*" The Plains Indian was a tough foe. Kiowa Chief Sitting Bear was captured in 1871 while raiding Texas settlements at the age of 70. Shackled at the wrists and ankles, he somehow managed to acquire and conceal a hunting knife. He freed himself by stripping the flesh off of his hands with his teeth and then knifing the escort guards in his wagon before he was shot dead.

McCLERNAND

GODFREY

LONG

THE NEZ PERCES AT BEAR PAW MOUNTAIN

The three-year old Sioux war for the Black Hills had ended in the spring of 1877, and George Custer was buried at West Point. Sitting Bull, the Hunkpappa Sioux chief, had fled into Canada. O. O. Howard, the army commander in the northwest territory, opposed the recently approved relocation of the Nez Perces from the Wallowa valley in Washington to the reservation at Ft. Lapwai, Idaho. Following an ugly incident that resulted in four deaths, Chief Joseph fled with 300 of his Nez Perces warriors who were known to be crack marksmen and 500 women and children, hoping to join either the Crows in Montana or Sitting Bull's Sioux in Canada. Pursuing troops from Ft. Lapwai were routed at White Bird Creek with 34 killed. Thus began a three-month campaign chasing the Nez Perces over 1,700 miles of exceptionally rugged terrain. Battles were fought at Clearwater on July 11th; at Big Hole River on August 9th, resulting in 71 more army casualties; and at Camas Meadows on August 20th. Chief Joseph then crossed the Continental Divide, moving through the Yellowstone National Park, while managing to avoid 7th U.S. Cavalry units that were blocking the park's eastern exits. Moving north into Montana, the land of the Crows, he quickly discovered that the Crows had allied themselves with the army. He then continued north toward Canada, still looking for the Sioux. On September 13th, he repulsed an attack by the 7th U.S. Cavalry at Canyon Creek.

Howard ordered 400 additional troops stationed at Ft. Keogh to intercept the Nez Perces before they could enter Canada. Following a rapid march to the northwest, on September 30th the Nez Perces encampment was located on the Snake River, forty miles south of the Canadian border and on the edge of the Bear Paw Mountains. The commander, Nelson A. Miles, immediately attacked the camp with a four-mile cavalry charge by the 7th Cavalry. However, the charge was discovered early by the Indians and was repulsed and shattered with heavy losses. The casualties were fifty percent and included most of the officers. In later describing the charge Miles said, *"the gallop forward, preceding the charge, was one of the most brilliant and inspiring sights I have ever witnessed on any field."* Captain **Edward S. Godfrey** (Class of 1867), a 7th Cavalry squadron commander, and **Oscar F. Long** (Class of 1876), a 2nd lieutenant with the 5th Infantry Regiment, were in the frontal assault charge at the "Battle of Bear Paw Mountain", and both received the Medal of Honor. Godfrey's citation states that he *"led his command into action when he was severely wounded,"* and Long's citation states that *"having been directed to order a troop of cavalry to advance, and finding both its officers killed, he voluntarily assumed command, and under a heavy fire from the Indians advanced the troop to its proper position."*

In coordination with the cavalry charge, Miles also ordered a squadron of the 2nd U.S. Cavalry to circle the Nez Perces position to the west, where they captured most of Chief Joseph's pony herd and ran off 800 ponies. One troop of the squadron intercepted and engaged a force of 80 Nez Perces moving north, widely scattering them and rendering them ineffective. The citation of **Edward J. McClernand** (Class of 1870), a 2nd lieutenant, states that he *"gallantly attacked a band of hostiles and conducted the combat with excellent skill and boldness."* He was the third West Pointer awarded the Medal of Honor for heroism at the "Battle of Bear Paw Mountain". Chief Joseph surrendered following a six-day siege. In conversation with General Miles and his officers, he said "Hear me my chiefs! I am tired; my heart is sick and sad. From where the sun now stands, I will fight no more forever." Chief Joseph and 120 of his followers were subsequently relocated to the Ft. Colville Reservation on the Columbia River in Washington State.

37

THE UTES AT MILK CREEK

     In September of 1879, the Ute Indians were living on the Colorado White River Reservation, where an overly zealous agent named Nathan Meeker managed them. The Utes were horse borne nomads and very reluctant farmers. They did not appreciate the invasion of their lands by hordes of silver ore miners, and they forcefully refused Meeker's demand to slaughter their pony herds in order to increase the amount of available arable land. Irate Indians threatened him, and a frightened Meeker demanded army protection. An infantry-cavalry force under Thomas T. Thornburgh (Class of 1867) was quickly dispatched from Ft. Fred Steele, Wyoming. On September 29th, as Thornburgh forded Milk Creek on the northern border of the Ute reservation, 100 warriors blocked the trail leading into the reservation. A soldier's friendly wave of a hat was mistakenly perceived to be an unfriendly signal. A shot was fired and the "Battle of Milk Creek" began. A sharpshooter quickly killed Thornburgh while he was checking on his supply trains. His troops were besieged for a week until a messenger finally returned with a relief troop of the 9th U.S. Cavalry, following a twenty-three hour forced march. That relief troop was followed on October 5th by a larger force of four troops of the 5th U.S. Cavalry and five companies of the 4th Infantry Regiment, finally ending the siege. Meeker and nine agency employees had been killed during the engagement. His family and one other family were taken hostage by the Utes, who promptly disappeared into the mountains. Milk Creek became such an ugly national incident that the army ordered 1,500 troops onto the White River Reservation to attempt a forceful rescue of the hostages. On October 20th near the Ute encampment on the White River, **William P. Hall** (Class of 1868), a lieutenant with the 5th U. S. Cavalry, earned the Medal of Honor for his bravery. His citation reads that he "*With a reconnoitering party of 3 men, was attacked by 35 Indians and several times exposed himself to draw the fire of the enemy, giving his small party opportunity to reply with much effect.*" The next day special agent Charles Adams and Chief Ouray successfully negotiated the release of the hostages. Two years later the Ute tribe was relocated to Utah and southwestern Colorado.

THE OGLALA SIOUX AT O'FALLON'S CREEK

On March 24, 1880, a band of 30 to 40 Oglala Sioux of the Teton Tribes ran off 30 Crow Scout ponies at Ft. Custer. The 2nd U.S. Cavalry, commanded by John W. Davidson (Class of 1845), sent Troop M in "hot pursuit" of the raiders. They recaptured 16 of the ponies and returned to Ft. Custer. Troop C, temporarily located at Ft. Custer, took up the pursuit of the raiding Sioux with a four-day, 335 mile forced march that brought them to the banks of the Powder River on March 31st. Meanwhile, Troop E of the 2nd Cavalry had left Ft. Keogh, Montana, also scouting for hostile Sioux, and on March 31st they arrived on the banks of the Rosebud River after a six-day march. **Lloyd M. Brett** (Class of 1879), normally assigned to Troop A at Ft. Keogh, was on "detached service" to the under-strength Troop E. On April 1st, they broke camp and came upon the hostiles' trail crossing the Rosebud River in an easterly direction. Pursuing rapidly for 28 miles, they closed in on the unsuspecting Indian camp. On the Powder River, Troop C also broke camp on the morning of April 1st. The pursuit by the two troops converged and met near the fork of the Tongue River called O'Fallon's Creek. They attacked at 2:30 PM with a surprise charge that resulted in the capture of five braves and 46 horses, and the wounding of one brave. In a personal letter, Brett's troop commander wrote of his *"vigorous pursuit"*, and that he *"in the ensuing conflict exposed himself fearlessly, and but for positive orders to the contrary, would have charged into the stronghold of the Indians."* Both Generals Nelson Miles and Thomas W. Terry recommended Brett for the Medal of Honor. His citation reads: *"For most distinguished gallantry in action against hostile Sioux Indians near O'Fallon's Creek, Montana, on April 1, 1880, by fearless exposure and dashing bravery in cutting off the Indians' pony herd, thereby greatly crippling the hostiles, while second lieutenant, 2nd Cavalry."* Brett went on to fight against the Cree and the Apache Indians. He received the surrender of Santiago City in the *Spanish American War* and fought the Moros in the *Philippine Insurrection*. As a brigadier general, he commanded the 160th Brigade of the 80th Division in *World War I*. In 1924, Brett was the Commander-in-Chief of the Veterans of Foreign Wars.

CHIEF VICTORIO AT LAS ANIMAS CANYON

In the southwest, there had been four years of relative peace with the Apache tribes since George Crook's (Class of 1852) "Arizona Campaign" ended with the "Battle of Turret Peak" in March of 1873. The great Chiricahua Apache Chief Cochise had died in 1874, and in 1875, the government decided to abolish four of the Arizona reservations and to consolidate all of the Apache tribes at the notorious San Carlos Reservation. San Carlos was well known as "an awful place: barren, hot, disease ridden." It was in the terrible misery and discontent of the San Carlos Reservation that Victorio, a Warm Springs Apache, and later Geronimo, a Chiricahua Apache known as "The Power", rose to positions of leadership, following in the footsteps of Mangas Coloradas and Cochise. On September 2nd, 1877, Victorio led over 300 warriors out of the San Carlos Reservation. Pursued vigorously, he surrendered a month later at Ft. Wingate, New Mexico, 200 miles to the northwest. Ordered to return to San Carlos, Victorio managed to escape into the mountains with 80 warriors, hoping to return to his homeland of Ojo Caliente in New Mexico. On September 4th, 1879, the *Victorio War* began when he and 60 warriors raided the horse herd camp of Troop E, 9th U.S. Cavalry, killing eight soldiers and capturing 46 horses. His force rapidly grew to 150 warriors as he raided the entire southwest territory and the State of Chihuahua in Mexico.

Two Military Academy graduates from the Class of 1877 were awarded the Medal of Honor for bravery against Victorio's force at Las Animas Canyon, New Mexico, on September 18th, 1879. Both were 2nd lieutenants assigned to the 9th U.S. Cavalry, a regiment of black enlisted men led by white officers. Its sister regiment, the 10th Cavalry, was the first to be called the "Buffalo Soldiers" by the Indians. Both of these regiments successfully fought the Apaches and Comanches for ten years. One commander stated, "They follow wherever led, they will go without leading, and will stay with their leader through all danger and never desert him." **Mathias W. Day** was cited for his conduct as he "*Advanced alone into the enemy's lines and carried off a wounded soldier of his command under a hot fire and after he had been ordered to retreat.*" **Robert T. Emmet** was cited as follows: "*Lt. Emmet was in G Troop, which was sent to relieve a detachment of soldiers under attack by hostile Apaches. During a flank attack on the Indian camp, made to divert the hostiles, Lt. Emmet and 5 of his men became surrounded when the Indians returned to defend their camp. Finding that the Indians were making for a position from which they could direct their fire on the retreating troop, the Lieutenant held his point with his party until the soldiers reached the safety of a canyon. Lt. Emmet then continued to hold his position while his party recovered their horses. The enemy force consisted of approximately 200.*" Victorio continued to fight for another year until he was finally killed at Tres Castillon by Mexican troops under Joaquin Terrazos in October of 1880. Terrazos' after-action report simply stated that "The indian Victorio is of the dead." Chief Nana led a few of the survivors back to New Mexico, where he would later join Geronimo – "The Power".

CHIEF NANA'S RAID AND THE BATTLE AT CIBICUE CREEK

The seventy-year old Nana, the last great Chief of the Warm Springs Apaches, had escaped with the other survivors of Tres Castillon. Hiding by day and riding at night, he gradually rebuilt the Apache force. A young Chihenne warrior who rode with Nana, James Kaywaykla, referred to the Apache God Ussen when he said of Nana, "Ussen had not commanded that we love our enemies; Nana did not love his; and he was not content with an eye for an eye, nor a life for a life. For every Apache killed he took many lives." A scout returned with word that 100 Chihenne women and children captured at Tres Castillon were to be sold as slaves by the Mexicans. In June of 1881, Nana began his war of retribution. It would be called *Nana's Raid*, and "Of all the extraordinary deeds of war ever performed ... this was arguably the most brilliant." Starting with a force of 15 warriors that never exceeded 40, the July and August raids averaged 50 miles a day, "won seven serious battles with cavalry", and attacked over a dozen towns and settlements while being pursued by more than 1,400 soldiers. "The lightening mobility of the raiders dumbfounded New Mexicans." On August 16th, **George R. Burnett** (Class of 1880), a lieutenant with the 9th U.S. Cavalry, earned the Medal of Honor for his bravery against Nana in the Cuchillo Negro Mountains of New Mexico. His citation states that he "*saved the life of a dismounted soldier, who was in imminent danger of being cut off, by alone galloping to his assistance under a heavy fire and escorting him to a place of safety, his horse being twice shot in this action.*" In the autumn, Nana holed up in Sonora, Mexico, and soon joined his brother-in-law Geronimo at the "Stronghold", which was deep in the Sierra Madre Mountains.

Meanwhile at the San Carlos and the White Mountain Reservations in the summer of 1881, Geronimo had come under the influence of a medicine man named Nakaidoklinni. "The Dreamer" predicted the resurrection of the dead and "that the whites would soon vanish from Apache country." His movement was one of several popular *Ghost Dances*, a new religion that was spreading among the tribes in the 1880's. The Ft. Apache commander, Eugene A. Carr (Class of 1850), was urged by the San Carlos agent J. C. Tiffany, "a man already infamous for his corrupt tactics", to send troops to the two reservations. Failing to hear from two scouts he had sent to Cibicue Creek, where a series of *Ghost Dances* were then being held, Carr arrived there on August 30th with a force of 79 troopers and 23 White Mountain Apache scouts. He promptly arrested Nakaidoklinni and hurriedly prepared to escort him to Ft. Apache for an investigation. Carr marched along Cibicue Creek with 100 Apaches moving parallel to his route, trying to ensure that "no harm came to 'The Dreamer'." He encamped late in the afternoon, and the Apaches moved in closer, increasing the tension. The chief scout later said, "*the interpreter not knowing enough of the Indian language*" made "*a fatal blunder*". A captain waved off the Apaches and a shot was fired. The ensuing battle lasted until dark. Geronimo and his sister Lozen were among the Apaches that fought at Cibicue Creek. All of the Apache army scouts deserted and turned on Carr's troops, the only recorded instance of Apache scouts mutinying. Seven troopers were killed and 55 horses were taken. **William H. Carter** (Class of 1873), a 6th U.S. Cavalry lieutenant, was awarded the Medal of Honor when he "*rescued, with the voluntary assistance of two soldiers, the wounded from under a heavy fire.*" Two days later, Ft. Apache was attacked in "an unprecedented action from warriors who preferred the quicksilver tactics of guerilla combat."

44

FIGHTING THE WARM SPRINGS AND WHITE MOUNTAIN APACHES

In the spring of 1882, an Apache war party bent on recruiting warriors stormed the San Carlos Reservation hoping to recruit the Warm Springs Apaches of Ojo Caliente to join in their fight. They struck on April 4th, killed the police chief and were able to recruit several hundred new followers. Moving south toward Mexico they raided extensively and killed 30 to 50 settlers. Five troops of the 4th U.S. Cavalry and a unit of scouts aggressively pursued the raiding war party. On April 23rd, a patrol came upon the raiders holed up in Horseshoe Canyon in the Peloncillo Mountains of New Mexico. They immediately attacked, but the Apaches were able to escape after killing five troopers and wounding seven. **Wilber E. Wilder** (Class of 1877), a 1st lieutenant with the 4th Cavalry, was awarded the Medal of Honor for his bravery when he *"assisted, under a heavy fire, to rescue a wounded comrade."* Two troops of the 6th U.S. Cavalry quickly reinforced the 4th Cavalry troops, and the pursuit continued into the State of Chihuahua in Mexico. On April 28th, they again located and attacked a strong Apache defensive position in the mountains, and again they failed. The cavalry force finally withdrew after using up most of its ammunition. Their aggressive pursuit and the attack of the Apaches in Mexico caused serious political repercussions from an angry Mexican government.

On July 6th, Chief Natiotish, a White Mountain Apache, led a small war party back to the San Carlos Reservation where they killed eight Indian police, including the new police chief, and freed 60 of his tribe. The reinforced band then proceeded to raid throughout the Tonto Basin. Fourteen troops of cavalry began a thorough search of the countryside between Ft. Apache and Ft. Verde near General Springs. Natiotish, trying to annihilate a pursuing troop of the 6th U.S. Cavalry, prepared an elaborate ambush by concealing his warriors along the edge of a deep and narrow canyon. The canyon, often incorrectly called the Big Dry Fork and Big Dry Wash, is located on a branch of East Clear Creek on the Mogollon Rim in Arizona. The ambush was discovered, however, by an alert army scout, and the commander, Adna R. Chaffee, was quickly reinforced with two troops from the 3rd U.S. Cavalry and two additional troops from the 6th U.S. Cavalry. Chaffee established a base of fire from the opposite side of the canyon, while two troops of cavalry simultaneously struck both of the Apache flanks. The aggressive cavalry attack carried the position, killing 26 warriors and wounding the rest. Three Military Academy graduates were cited for heroism in this action and received the Medal of Honor. **Thomas Cruse** (Class of 1879), a 2nd lieutenant with the 6th U.S. Cavalry, *gallantly charged hostile Indians, and with his carbine compelled a party of them to keep under cover of their breastworks, thus being enabled to recover a severely wounded soldier."* **George H. Morgan** (Class of 1880), a 2nd lieutenant with the 3rd U.S. Cavalry, *"gallantly held his ground at a critical moment and fired upon the advancing enemy (hostile Indians) until himself disabled by a shot."* **Frank West** (Class of 1872), a 1st lieutenant with the 6th U.S. Cavalry, *"rallied his command and led it in the advance against the enemy's fortified position."* The surviving Indians were returned to the San Carlos Reservation. The battle at Horseshoe Canyon ended all future White Mountain Apache raids. Only the Chiricahuas and the Warm Springs Apaches led by Geronimo remained to be pacified in the southwest.

CLARK MAUS

46

CHIEF GERONIMO AND THE SIERRA MADRE CAMPAIGN

In the summer of 1885, Geronimo, "the wickedest Indian that ever lived", was loose in the Sierra Madre Mountains of Mexico. General Crook secured every border water hole with troop size units searching daily for infiltrating Chiricahuas. He ordered two companies led by Emmet Crawford and Britton Davis (Class of 1881) to pursue Geronimo into Mexico. Mexican troops were also searching independently for Geronimo, but he eluded everyone. Finally, in December Crook sent Crawford and three other officers into Mexico with 100 Indian scouts organized into two companies. A scout soon reported that Geronimo was encamped near the head of the Aros River in mountains known as the "Devil's Backbone", the "roughest region in all Mexico." Undetected, Crawford marched through the night and attacked Geronimo's camp at dawn on January 10th, seizing all of his supplies. Early on the next day, a large force that Crawford believed to be reinforcements from General Crook approached his camp. In reality it was one of the Mexican units that were also pursuing Geronimo. They mistook Crawford's scouts for hostile Apaches and opened fire. Crawford waved a handkerchief as he moved forward to a rock promontory and shouted, "Soldados Americanos!" A Mexican shot rang out, and **Marion P. Maus** (Class of 1874), a 1st Lieutenant and the second in command, turned to see Crawford *"lying on the rocks with a wound in his head and some of his brains upon the rock."* Later, after a two hour battle with the Apaches on January 11th, Geronimo was driven deeper into the mountains. Maus was awarded the Medal of Honor and cited for *"most distinguished gallantry in action with hostile Apaches led by Geronimo and Natchez."*

The Sierra Madre was no longer a safe sanctuary and the Chiricahua Apache morale was at a low point. Chief Nana surrendered, and on March 25th Geronimo met with Crook at Canyon de los Embudos, twenty miles south of the border. That night Crook wrote that they were "as fierce as so many tigers," but they had decided to surrender. Crook returned alone to Ft. Bowie, and the rest of the party headed north. However, on the evening of March 28th the entire band of Indians got drunk on mescal; and 18 warriors, 13 women, and 6 children led by Geronimo and Cochise's son Naiche, fled from the camp. Maus immediately pursued, but an embarrassed Crook requested that he be reassigned following "eight years of the hardest work of my life." Geronimo then began a five month 1886 summer campaign that "can fairly be regarded as the most remarkable campaign of guerilla warfare ever witnessed on the North American continent." They were a desperate group. Naiche said, "We saw that we were in for it and would probably be killed anyway." Geronimo said, "We were reckless with our lives ... so we gave no quarter to anyone and asked no favors." General Miles mobilized 5,000 troops, a quarter of the entire army, as the Apaches scattered into small raiding groups that moved east and north. Geronimo's group of six men, possibly including Naiche, began their last raid, going as far north as Ojo Caliente. On April 27th, they struck Peck's Ranch in southern Arizona looking for ammunition. *"It was the need for ammunition that motivated the Chiricahua raids.... Mexican cartridges could not always be used with the Winchester and Springfield rifles the Apaches coveted."* A troop of the 10th U.S. Cavalry pursued one group returning to Mexico, and on May 3rd, cornered it in the Pinto Mountains. **Powhatan H. Clarke** (Class of 1884), a 2nd lieutenant, was cited for bravery during a brisk skirmish, when he *"rushed forward to the rescue of a soldier who was severely wounded and lay, disabled, exposed to the enemy's fire and carried him to a place of safety."* On September 4, 1886, Geronimo finally surrendered at Skeleton Canyon southeast of Ft. Bowie, and four days later the Chiricahuas were entrained for Florida as the 4th U.S Cavalry band played *Auld Lang Syne.*

47

GARLINGTON

GRESHAM

ROBERT A. GETZ 49©

48

THE MINICONJOUS SIOUX AT WOUNDED KNEE CREEK

The *Ghost Dance* religion infected the several Sioux tribes in the spring of 1890. It was an "Indian Holy War" inspired by the Nevada "messiah" Wovoka of the Paiute tribe. In 1890, the new religion erupted at the White River Agency, where Chief Sitting Bull's Hunkpappa Sioux lived on the Standing Rock Reservation, and where Chief Big Foot led the Miniconjous Sioux on the Cheyenne River Reservation. On December 15th, agency Indian police quietly arrested Sitting Bull as he slept in his teepee at Standing Rock for allegedly leading the *Ghost Dance*. As they prepared to take him south to the Pine Ridge Reservation, his excited followers caused a wild melee that resulted in Sitting Bull's death. Many of the Indians then fled to the Cheyenne River Reservation hoping to join Chief Big Foot, but he had also fled with 350 of his tribe, hoping to reach Chief Red Cloud's Oglala Sioux on the Pine Ridge Reservation. General Miles thought that Chief Big Foot was headed for the "Stronghold", an Indian redoubt area on the edge of Pine Ridge, and sent four troops of the 7th U.S. Cavalry in pursuit. They intercepted the Miniconjous at Porcupine Creek and escorted the 120 braves and 230 women and children to a camp on Wounded Knee Creek. James W. Forsyth (Class of 1856) was ordered to disarm Chief Big Foot's band and to march them to the railroad for movement to Omaha. In the darkness of early morning more 7th Cavalry troops arrived, and the Indian camp was soon surrounded by 500 additional troops and four rapid-fire Hotchkiss cannon. After breakfast, the tepees were searched in a second weapons shakedown, and the confiscated weapons, which included axes and knives, were placed in piles. Two more rifles were found, including a new Winchester that belonged to a young Miniconjous Sioux named Black Coyote. Black Coyote raised the rifle over his head as troopers grabbed at him, and a shot rang out. It was never determined whether Black Coyote had deliberately fired his rifle, or if it was accidentally fired, or if a soldier scuffling with Black Coyote had fired the shot. It was later recalled that a warrior named Black Fox had leaped to his feet and had begun firing a rifle. Regardless of how the fight began, vicious and confused hand-to-hand fighting immediately broke out. The Hotchkiss cannon shelled the camp from the high ground, killing troopers and Indians alike. When the firing finally ended, there were over 170 dead Sioux Indians, 31 dead troopers, and 39 wounded troopers. Most of the army casualties were the result of friendly bullets and shrapnel from the Hotchkiss cannon. It is still a false and misleading sentiment, dignifying conspiracy and honoring treachery", and also that "'Wounded Knee' may be a lovely phrase. It was not the soldier's guilt and the warrior's victimization." Two members of the Class of 1876, both 1st lieutenants with the 7th U.S. Cavalry, were decorated with the Medal of Honor for their heroism at Wounded Knee Creek on December 29, 1890. **Ernest A. Garlington** was cited for his "*distinguished gallantry*", and **John C. Gresham** "*voluntarily led a party into a ravine to dislodge Sioux Indians concealed therein. He was wounded during this action.*" Both officers later fought in the *Spanish American War* and the *Philippine Insurrection*. Garlington was appointed the Army Inspector General from 1906 to 1917.

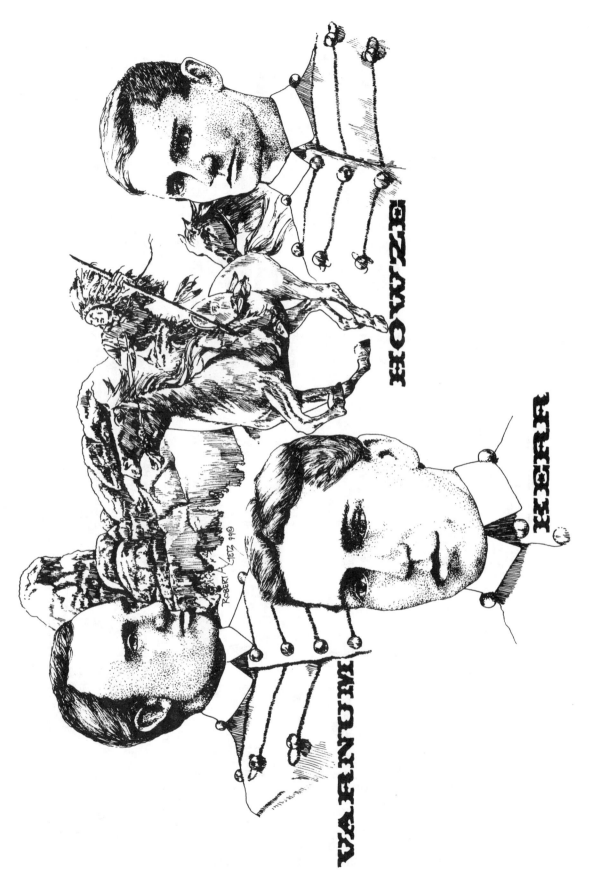

THE BATTLES AT WHITE RIVER AND WHITE CLAY CREEK

On December 30th of 1890, one day after the "Battle at Wounded Knee", the 7th U.S. Cavalry was ambushed at White Clay Creek near the Pine Ridge Indian Agency. Elements of the 9th U.S. Cavalry immediately came to their rescue, and together they were able to extricate themselves and to withdraw. Captain **Charles A. Varnum** (Class of 1872), commanding Troop B of the 7th Cavalry, received the Medal of Honor for heroism on that day. Varnum's citation states *"While executing an order to withdraw, seeing that a continuation of the movement would expose another troop of his regiment to being cut off and surrounded, he disregarded orders to retire, placed himself in front of his men, led a charge upon the advancing Indians, regained a commanding position that had just been vacated, and thus insured a safe withdrawal of both detachments without further loss."* Varnum, who had been wounded at the "Battle of the Little Big Horn", was retired for disability in 1907. He later was returned to active duty and served as a colonel in World War I.

Two days later on the White River in South Dakota, the 6th U.S. Cavalry encountered a large force of warriors attempting to escape from the Pine Ridge Reservation and enter the "Bad Lands". Captain **John B. Kerr** (Class of 1870), 6th U.S. Cavalry, was in pursuit of this band and was awarded the Medal of Honor for his bravery on January 1st of 1891. Kerr's citation reads: *"For distinguished bravery while in command of his troop in action against hostile Sioux Indians on the north bank of the White River, near the mouth of Little Grass Creek, South Dakota, where he defeated a force of 300 Brule Sioux warriors, and turned the Sioux tribe, which was endeavoring to enter the 'Bad Lands', back into the Pine Ridge Agency."* Kerr went on to fight at Santa Cruz in Cuba in the *Spanish American War*, where he was awarded the Silver Star. He retired as a brigadier general in 1909. Also in this same battle at White River was 2nd lieutenant **Robert L. Howze** (Class of 1888), a 2nd lieutenant with Troop K of the 6th U.S. Cavalry, whose citation simply reads: *"Bravery in action."* Howze also fought at Santa Cruz and in the *Philippine Insurrection*, and was awarded the Silver Star in both conflicts. He rose to the rank of major general and commanded the 36th Division of the American Expeditionary Force in World War I.

The Sioux formally surrendered at White Clay Creek on January 15th of 1891, and were returned peacefully to the Pine Ridge Reservation. The *Ghost Dance* uprising and its several peripheral actions were at an end. The battles at White River and at White Clay Creek, closely following the battle at Wounded Knee Creek, were essentially the last serious confrontations. The *Indian Wars* were finally concluded.

51

THE SPANISH AMERICAN WAR

THE BATTLES FOR EL CANEY AND SAN JUAN RIDGE IN CUBA

In February 1898, "Remember the Maine! To hell with Spain!" was the rallying call of 200,000 volunteers seeking to avenge the sinking of the battleship *U.S.S. Maine* in Havana Harbor. Congress declared war in April, and an expeditionary force landed in June. The city of Santiago was defended by Spanish troops entrenched on the San Juan Hill-Kettle Hill ridge complex, with the village of El Caney on its northern flank. The capture of El Caney would secure the American army's right flank and facilitate the seizure of the entire ridge complex. On July 1st, the army attacked along a wide front in oppressive heat and high humidity. As the 17th U.S. Infantry moved over the ridge's crest and deployed, *"they were struck by killing volleys from the trenches. The regimental commander was hit three times"*, and the regiment withdrew into a nearby hollow. The sniper fire from trenches on the high ground to their front was deadly. Six hundred Spaniards defended El Caney from the trenches, led by their heroic leader General Joaquin del Ray. The 17th Infantry attacked three times and sustained heavy losses. They finally secured the village with the assistance of supporting artillery in the late afternoon, long after Kettle Hill had been taken by Theodore Roosevelt's "Rough Riders". The regiment's casualties were 81 dead and 360 wounded. **Charles D. Roberts** (Class of 1897), a 2nd lieutenant with the 17th Infantry, was awarded the Medal of Honor for his heroism on July the 1st. His citation states that he *"Gallantly assisted in the rescue of the wounded from in front of the lines under heavy fire of the enemy."* Roberts was promoted to the rank of brigadier general before retiring.

Albert L. Mills (Class of 1879), a cavalry captain and a veteran of the Sioux *Indian Wars*, was with the U.S. Volunteers attacking the San Juan Ridge complex on July 1st. Mills was awarded the Medal of Honor for his *"Distinguished gallantry in encouraging those near him by his bravery and coolness after being shot through the head and entirely without sight."* He permanently lost the use of an eye in this fight. Mill's next assignment was as the Superintendent of the Military Academy from 1898 to 1906. He retired in 1916 as a major general.

52

HEARD

WELBORN

Robert A. Getz 99©

THE FIGHT FOR SANTIAGO AND THE DEFENSE OF THE *U.S.S. WANDERER*

With the San Juan Heights having been secured the previous day, the army prepared to continue the attack on Santiago the next morning. That night the troops dug in along the ridge and attempted to resupply in spite of the many flooding streams, swollen from the incessant heavy rain throughout the night. The troops had been sleepless for two days while under fire, and they were near collapse from exhaustion, having been greatly "weakened by the fierce tropical sun." Throughout the night, the "*Spanish kept up a severe continuous drumbeat of rifle fire*" with sharpshooters concealed in the tall grass. Theodore Roosevelt later commented that "*As the day wore on, the fight, though raging fitfully at intervals, gradually died away.*" **Ira C. Welborn** (Class of 1898), a 2nd lieutenant with the 9th U.S. Infantry, was awarded the Medal of Honor for his heroism on July 2nd, when he "*Voluntarily left shelter and went to the aid of a private of his company who was wounded.*"

On the 23rd of July, **John W. Heard** (Class of 1883), a 1st lieutenant with the 3rd U.S. Cavalry, was awarded the Medal of Honor for heroism while on the transport ship *U.S.S. Wanderer* at the mouth of the Manimani River, west of Bahia Honda. On July 16th, the ship had sailed from the United States with troops of the 3rd Cavalry and was positioned at the Manimani River, just west of a naval blockade of the northern Cuban coastline. The blockade stretched east from Bahia Honda to Havana and then to Cardenas. In defending his ship which was under attack by Spaniards, Heard's citation states that "*After two men had been shot down by Spaniards while transmitting orders to the engine room on the 'Wanderer', the ship having become disabled, this officer took the position held by them and personally transmitted the orders, remaining at his post until the ship was out of danger.*"

THE CHINA RELIEF EXPEDITION

THE BATTLES AT TIENTSIN AND PEKING

In the spring of 1900, the "Boxers", "violent Chinese Nationalists who wanted to drive out the 'foreign devils'", besieged the western embassies in Peking. U.S. Secretary of State John Hay had proposed an "Open Door" trade policy. China opposed this policy as well as "spheres of western influence" in China. The "Boxer" society was called "The Righteous Harmony Fists". Their insignia was a "clenched fist", and their mystic belief, like that of the American Indian "Ghost Dancers", held that they were immune to bullets. In late June, an American force consisting of the 9th U.S. Infantry Regiment and a battalion of marines sailed from Manila in the Philippines and landed at Taku near Tientsin, where they were reinforced by troops under General Chaffee. The American force numbered 2,500 in a total international force of 6,000 troops. On July 13th, they attacked Tientsin, a walled city and a strategic barrier to Peking, which was 75 miles distant. The battle to breach the two walls encircling Tientsin lasted 15 hours. The 9th Infantry finally broke through both walls, entered the city, and were quickly caught in a brutal crossfire. When the color-bearer fell, the regimental commander, Colonel Emerson Liscum, seized the colors and continued moving forward. Moments later he fell mortally wounded while shouting, "Keep up the fire!" This later became the battle cry of the 9th Infantry, whose members are now nicknamed "The Manchus". **Louis B. Lawton** (Class of 1893), a 1st lieutenant with the 9th Infantry, was awarded the Medal of Honor when he "*Carried a message and guided reinforcements across a wide and fire-swept space, during which he was thrice wounded.*"

The attack was continued and several more engagements were fought before the army reached Peking's city gates on August 12th. The international army now numbered 18,600. On August 14th the gates of the outer city were secured. Two American companies then scaled the "Tartar Wall" and provided covering fire to an attacking British brigade. A trumpeter with the 14th U. S. Infantry received the Medal of Honor for his heroism on the "Tartar Wall", when his colonel called for volunteers to scale the city wall. **Calvin P. Titus**, musician trumpeter of the 14th Infantry, responded, "*I'll try sir!*" and "*with no ropes or ladders Titus worked his way up the thirty foot wall by finding handholds and footholds amid the stones*", inspiring his fellow soldiers. Titus' citation states that he displayed "*Gallant and daring conduct in the presence of his colonel and other officers and enlisted men of his regiment; was first to scale the wall of the city.*" Titus later entered the Military Academy, graduating in 1905. In 1902, he received his Medal of Honor from President Theodore Roosevelt in the newly completed Cullum Hall during the Military Academy's June Week Centennial Celebration. After the fall of Peking, China's dowager empress sued for peace, and formal trade agreements between China and the western powers were reinstated.

THE PHILIPPINE INSURRECTION

While Cuba and the sinking of the battleship *U.S.S. Maine* in Havana harbor were the primary focus of attention by Americans during the *Spanish American War*, the War Department dispatched Admiral George Dewey's Asiatic Squadron to the Philippine Islands, where a large Spanish fleet was based in Manila harbor. Arriving on the morning of May 1st of 1898, Dewey observed the Spanish fleet while standing on the deck of his flagship *U.S.S. Olympia*. He quickly gave his now famous order "You may fire when ready, Gridley!" By noon of that day his squadron had sunk ten major Spanish warships with no American fatalities. The besieged Spanish garrison in Manila surrendered to Dewey on August 14th. A series of bloody and ruthless events then began that are summarized best by the statement that "The Spanish War had been short and glorious, and easily understood. The Philippine War was long and ugly ...." The recently arrived American troops and the Filipino rebel commander, Emilio Aguinaldo, initially cooperated to force the surrender of the many isolated Spanish garrisons based in Manila and throughout the islands. On December 10th, the United States signed a treaty with Spain that ceded Guam and Puerto (Porto) Rico to the United States; granted Cuba its freedom; and allowed the purchase of the Philippine Islands by the United States for $20 million. However, relations between Dewey and Aguinaldo were sharply deteriorating during late 1898 and early 1899. Aguinaldo's memoirs relate that Admiral Dewey had said to him "America is rich in territory and money, and needs no colonies ...," and I "have no doubt whatever about the recognition of Philippine independence by the United States." Whether or not Dewey actually made these statements to Aguinaldo is not historically clear and is certainly debatable, but Aguinaldo later believed that he had been lied to and this became the basis for what led to the *Philippine Insurrection*. The strong Filipino desire for independence, previously directed against the Spaniards for so many years, was now directed against their perceived new oppressors - the Americans. In the first half of 1899, town after town on the island of Luzon fell to advancing American troops. As the rebels withdrew deep into the jungles of the interior, stunned by American firepower and tactics, a new phase of the *Philippine Insurrection* began - an ugly "Guerilla Warfare" phase. Aguinaldo was inaugurated as the first President of the Philippines at the town of Maldos on July 23, 1899, and for two years he led his "Insurrectos" in some of the most brutal fighting against American troops ever recorded.

THE FIGHTS AT SAN MIGUEL AND THE ZAPOTE BRIDGE IN LUZON

In late April of 1899, Brigadier General Henry Lawton's "Northern Expedition" began an attack toward San Isidro. To cover his advance he ordered a detachment of scouts consisting of twenty-five sharpshooters under William H. Young, his Chief of Scouts and a former frontiersman, to reconnoiter ahead of his force. By May 13th, because of fatigue and exhaustion, only ten were able to continue the march. Two officers had joined Young the previous day, one of whom was **William E. Birkhimer** (Class of 1870), a captain with the 3rd U.S. Artillery. His instructions were "*to use the scouts as necessary*"; "*to investigate the road to the enemy left and rear for a possible turning movement*"; and to "*look up good artillery positions.*" The twelve men approached San Miguel de Mayumo at 9:00 A.M. on the 13th, where they encountered a force of 300 Filipinos in well-dug trenches. Five scouts moved to the left flank, while Young and Birkhimer "*gallantly and desperately charged the center of the line, unhesitantly followed ...*" by the others. It took 30 minutes to cover the 150 yards to the trenches, where they found 49 dead defenders. Young, a civilian, was killed in this assault. Birkhimer and the ten other scouts were all recommended for the Medal of Honor. Birkhimer's citation states that he "*With 12 men charged and routed 300 of the enemy.*"

On June 10th, General Lawton's "Paranque Campaign" penetrated the "Insurrecto" center, and he quickly moved to attack their rear areas. He reported in a situation report that "Fighting has been severe" and "heat terrific ... will move over to Paranque tonight; no good water all day, which accounts for much suffering." On June 13th, he reported that the troops had a "*severe engagement today with enemy in strong entrenchments at crossing Zapote River near Bacoor, Cavite Province.*" The enemy were "*driven from heavy and well constructed entrenchments to which they held tenaciously; their loss several hundred.*" This fight, with gunboats in the Bay providing supporting fire, "*developed into the hardest fight since the hostilities with the Filipinos began.*" **William H. Sage** (Class of 1882), a captain with the 23rd U.S. Infantry, was there. His citation reads that he "*With nine men volunteered to hold an advanced position and held it against a terrific fire of the enemy, estimated at 1,000 strong. Taking a rifle from a wounded man, and cartridges from the belts of others, Captain Sage himself killed five of the enemy.*"

MCGRATH

BELL

ROBERT A. GETZ 89 ©

THE FIGHTS AT CALAMBA AND ON THE ROAD TO PORAC

On July 26th of 1899, Brigadier General Robert H. Hall (Class of 1860) with a force of 1,000 soldiers "transported in launches and cascoes, gunboat accompanying" captured Calamba on the island of Luzon, an important strategic position at Laguna de Bay. Calamba had been an earlier objective of General Lawton's when he had captured Santa Cruz in April, but because of low shoal waters he had been unable to reach the town by boats. The 300 insurgents who now defended the town were finally driven away after sharp fighting. Forty Spanish prisoners of the insurgents were freed, and a serviceable Spanish gunboat was captured. **Hugh J. McGrath** (Class of 1880), a captain in the 4th U.S. Cavalry, received the Medal of Honor for his heroism at Calamba. His citation states that he "*Swam the San Juan River in the face of the enemy's fire and drove him from his entrenchments.*" McGrath was seriously wounded in a later action on October 8th and died from his wounds in a Manila hospital on November 7th. His Medal of Honor was awarded posthumously.

On September 9th, an insurgent force made a demonstration against the town of Santa Rita on the road to Porac. **James Franklin Bell** (Class of 1878), commanding the 36th Infantry, U.S. Volunteers, was cited as follows for his bravery: "*While in advance of his regiment charged seven insurgents with his pistol and compelled the surrender of the captain and two privates under a close fire from the remaining insurgents concealed in a bamboo thicket.*" Bell was also awarded the Distinguished Service Cross for heroism in the Philippines and was later promoted to major general.

LOGAN

PARKER

Robert A. Getz
99EJ

THE ATTACK AT SAN JACINTO AND THE DEFENSE OF VIGAN

On November 9th of 1899, General Lloyd Wheaton's troops were transported by ship to Nagasaki on Luzon's Lingayan Gulf. The very next day they found themselves immediately engaged by insurgents near San Fabian. A battalion of the 33rd U.S. Infantry attacked and defeated the 400 entrenched insurgents. A day later on the 11th, Wheaton was preparing to attack San Jacinto when he again made contact near there with more insurgents. A second battalion of the 33rd Infantry under Major **John A. Logan, Jr.** (ex-cadet of the Class of 1887) attacked 1,200 entrenched insurgents, resulting in the loss of his life and that of 6 enlisted men. Logan's posthumous Medal of Honor citation reads: "*For most distinguished gallantry in leading his battalion upon the entrenchments of the enemy, on which occasion he fell mortally wounded.*"

On December 4th, 800 insurgents attacked a small garrison at Vigan in Luzon, which was under the command of Lt. Col. **James Parker** (Class of 1876) of the 45th U.S. Infantry. A situation report characterized his total force as: "*consisting of "B" Company and 153 sick and foot-sore men Thirty-third Infantry.*" The insurgents attacked at 4:00 A.M.. An "after-action" report summarized Parker's successful defense as: "*entering the city in darkness; severe street fighting ensued; continued four hours; enemy driven out, leaving behind 40 dead, 32 prisoners, including many officers, and 84 rifles. Now on outskirts entrenching.*" A relief force under General Young arrived on the evening of December 5th, after first overcoming insurgents 12 miles south of Vigan. Parker was awarded the Medal of Honor and cited as follows: "*While in command of a small garrison repulsed a savage night attack by overwhelming numbers of the enemy, fighting at close quarters in the dark for several hours.*"

ROBERT A. GETZ 99©

VAN SCHAICK

CHASING INSURGENTS IN BATANGAS

Emilio Aguinaldo finally was captured during a high-risk clandestine operation, in which American officers posed as the prisoners of friendly Filipino soldiers who represented themselves as "Insurrectos", thereby gaining access to Aguinaldo's secret camp. On April 16th of 1901, the captured Aguinaldo took an oath of allegiance to the United States, but the guerilla fighting continued for another full year. On November 23rd, **Louis Van Schaick** (ex-cadet of the Class of 1900), a 1st lieutenant with the 4th U.S. Infantry, was awarded the Medal of Honor for his heroism near Nasugbu in Batangas Province, while he was in hot pursuit of a band of guerillas. Van Schaik's citation reads: "*While in pursuit of a band of insurgents was the first of his detachment to emerge from a canyon, and seeing a column of insurgents and fearing they might turn and dispatch his men as they emerged one by one from the canyon, galloped forward and closed with the insurgents, thereby throwing them into confusion until the arrival of others of the detachment.*" President Woodrow Wilson personally presented to Van Schaick his Medal of Honor. The insurrection was almost over, and on July 4th of 1902, President Theodore Roosevelt declared the *Philippine Insurrection* ended and granted a general amnesty. Five thousand Americans and twenty thousand Filipinos had either been killed, or had died of wounds or disease during the insurrection.

60

FIGHTING THE MOROS IN THE PHILIPPINES

wilson

Kennedy

Following the conclusion of the *Philippine Insurrection*, only the Moros, "a savage primitive people", continued their rebellion, which had begun many years earlier against the Spaniards on the islands of Samar, Patian, and Mindanao. An expedition to the Patian Islands was organized in 1909 to either kill or apprehend a Moro bandit named Jikiri, "who took refuge with his party in a cave" before finally being routed and destroyed. This action resulted in two Military Academy graduates being awarded the Medal of Honor for their heroism on July the 4th of 1909. **Arthur Harrison Wilson** (Class of 1904), a 2nd lieutenant with the 6th U.S. Cavalry, was severely wounded by a barong that "*severed all of the muscles on one side of his neck.*" Wilson's citation states that he "*While in action against hostile Moros, when it being necessary to secure a mountain gun in position by rope and tackle, voluntarily with the assistance of an enlisted man, carried the rope forward and fastened it, being all the time under heavy fire of the enemy at short range.*" On the same day **John Thomas Kennedy** (Class of 1908), also a 2nd lieutenant in the 6th U.S. Cavalry, was cited as follows: "*While in action against hostile Moros, he entered with a few enlisted men the mouth of a cave occupied by a desperate enemy, this act having been ordered after he had volunteered several times. In this action 2nd Lt. Kennedy was severely wounded.*" Kennedy's injuries were "*almost fatal wounds whose partly visible scars he was to bear for the rest of his life.*" Kennedy's Medal of Honor was presented to him by President William H. Taft. He retired as a brigadier general in 1946.

61

THE CAPTURE OF VERA CRUZ IN MEXICO

ROBERT A. GETZ 99©

FRYER

In 1914, relations between Mexico and the United States had become very tense. In early April of that year, Mexican President Huerta's regime arrested American sailors from the *U.S.S. Dolphin*, who had gone ashore unarmed in Tampico. After being detained for two hours they were released by the Mexican Federal troops. Shortly after this incident, President Woodrow Wilson learned that a German ship loaded with arms and ammunition was approaching the Mexican port city of Vera Cruz. He immediately ordered the occupation of the town, and following a shelling, Vera Cruz was seized by U.S. Marines after a two day battle on the 21st and 22nd of April. The marine casualties totaled 19 killed and 47 wounded, while the combined Mexican losses in both defenders and civilians were 126 killed and 195 wounded. Captain **Eli Thompson Fryer** (ex-cadet of the Class of 1901) had joined the Marine Corps in 1900 and was a company commander at Vera Cruz. For his bravery in leading the assault by his marine company at Vera Cruz, he was awarded the Medal of Honor. His citation states: "*For distinguished conduct in battle, engagements of Vera Cruz, 21 and 22 April 1914. In both days' fighting at the head of his company, Captain Fryer was eminent and conspicuous in his conduct, leading his men with skill and courage.*" Fryer retired as a colonel in 1934, but was later returned to active duty. He retired again in 1941 as a brigadier general. The American occupation of Vera Cruz lasted until November 25, 1914. However, relations with Mexico continued to deteriorate and led to General John J. Pershing's (Class of 1886) punitive border expedition into Chihuahua against Pancho Villa on March 15, 1916.

WORLD WAR I AND THE SAN MIHIEL OFFENSIVE

PIKE

Under General John J. "Black Jack" Pershing, the "American Expeditionary Forces" (A.E.F.) had grown to seven divisions by mid-1918. Each division had been committed to combat as it arrived in Europe, but now they were ready to fight as a united American force on their own operational front. On September 12th, 500,000 A.E.F. soldiers began the St. Mihiel offensive, a double envelopment to eliminate a German salient. The 82nd Infantry Division initially had the mission of exerting pressure on the enemy by raiding and patrolling. However on the 13th, this mission was changed to one of protecting the flank of the 90th Infantry Division. The "*opposing positions in some places were only 20 yards apart, each of them being composed of wide zones of deep trenches, bristling with machine guns in concrete emplacements.*" The 82nd Division attacked after dark on the 13th, to a position that brought it on line with the 90th Division. On the 15th of September, the division continued its attack over terrain that was exposed to heavy artillery fire from the north, resulting in many casualties. Lt. Col. **Emory J. Pike** (Class of 1901), "*Going beyond the call of his own duties as Division Machine Gun Officer ... volunteered to assist in reorganizing advanced units under a terrific bombardment*", was posthumously awarded the Medal of Honor for his conduct near Vandieres. His citation reads: "*Having gone forward to reconnoiter new machine gun positions, Lt. Col. Pike offered his assistance in reorganizing advance infantry units which had become disorganized during a heavy artillery shelling. He succeeded in locating only about 20 men, but with these he advanced and when later joined by several infantry platoons rendered inestimable service in establishing outposts, encouraging all by his cheeriness, in spite of the extreme danger of the situation. When a shell had wounded one of the men in the outpost, Lt. Col. Pike immediately went to his aid and was severely wounded himself when another shell burst in the same place. While waiting to be brought to the rear, Lt. Col. Pike continued in command, still retaining his jovial manner of encouragement, directing the reorganization until the position could be held. The entire operation was carried on under terrific bombardment, and the example of courage and devotion to duty, as set by Lt. Col. Pike established the highest standard of morale and confidence to all under his charge. The wounds he received were the cause of his death.*"

WORLD WAR II

Nininger

THE BATAAN CAMPAIGN IN THE PHILIPPINES

On December 7th, 1941, America entered *World War II* after the Japanese navy attacked Pearl Harbor without warning. Days later the Japanese army landed on Luzon Island in the Philippines and advanced rapidly south into Bataan Province. During the "Bataan Campaign" **Alexander R. Nininger, Jr.** (Class of 1941) was awarded the *first* Medal of Honor in World War II for his heroism near Abucay on January 12, 1942. The award was posthumous. Nininger was a 2nd lieutenant with Company A, 57th Infantry, Philippine Division. The Japanese had driven a salient into the front lines of Company K, and snipers had infiltrated and occupied American foxholes, when Nininger reinforced the company with two squads from Company A. Filling his pockets with grenades and slinging a captured enemy light machine gun over his shoulder, he "*began a one-man assault on the enemy positions. Over and over he attacked them in their foxholes. He'd toss in a grenade and follow the blast with rapid bursts from his machine gun.*" He used an irrigation ditch to infiltrate enemy positions, while moving from tree to tree and flushing snipers. Company K rallied behind him and attacked, finding 20 enemy dead left by Nininger. They sighted him far ahead, still attacking through "*a hail of fire*" when he was hit by a bullet in the shoulder. "*He staggered, then caught himself and moved on, wiping out still another enemy foxhole.*" Out of grenades and continuing to advance, he was hit a second and a third time while using his rifle and bayonet. Nininger was last sighted wounded, staggering, and engaged in hand-to-hand combat with three enemy soldiers who attacked him with bayonets from behind. "*Whirling around, Nininger killed all three at point-blank range with his .45 caliber pistol before collapsing on the jungle floor.*" Nininger's citation reads: "*For conspicuous gallantry and intrepidity above and beyond the call of duty in action with the enemy near Abucay, Bataan, Philippine Islands on 12 January, 1942. This officer, though assigned to another company not then engaged in combat, voluntarily attached himself to Company K, same regiment, while that unit was being attacked by enemy force superior in firepower. Enemy snipers in trees and foxholes had stopped a counterattack to regain part of the position. In hand-to-hand fighting which followed, Lieutenant Nininger repeatedly forced his way to and into the hostile position. Though exposed to heavy enemy fire, he continued to attack with rifle and hand grenades and succeeded in destroying several enemy groups in foxholes and enemy snipers. Although wounded three times, he continued his attacks until he was killed after pushing alone far within the enemy position. When his body was found after recapture of the position, one enemy officer and two enemy soldiers lay dead around him.*" **Nininger Hall** at West Point was "dedicated to the perpetuation of the Cadet Honor Code."

MacArthur

A GENERAL PROMISES FINAL VICTORY

Few American soldiers have had as great an impact on the United States Military Academy, the American people, and the American military establishment as this recipient of the Medal of Honor. He was a great soldier who was first in his class at West Point, First Captain of the Corps of Cadets, fought in numerous wars, and was highly decorated. He was a Superintendent of the Military Academy and Chief of Staff of the Army prior to World War II. He was devoted to the principles of the Military Academy, and over six decades of service to his country he was the living personification of that institution's revered motto: "Duty, Honor, Country." **Douglas MacArthur** (Class of 1903), General U.S. Army, commanding U.S. Forces in the Far East, was awarded the Medal of Honor for his service to America in the heroic defense of Bataan. His March 25th, 1942, citation reads: "*For conspicuous leadership in preparing the Philippine Islands to resist conquest, for gallantry and intrepidity above and beyond the call of duty in action against invading Japanese forces, and for the heroic conduct of defensive and offensive operations on the Bataan Peninsula. He mobilized, trained, and led an army, which has received world acclaim for its gallant defense against a tremendous superiority of enemy forces in men and arms. His utter disregard of personal danger under heavy fire and aerial bombardment, his calm judgement in each crisis, inspired his troops, galvanized the spirit of resistance of the Filipino people, and confirmed the faith of the American people in their armed forces.*" On February 23rd, President Roosevelt personally ordered a reluctant MacArthur to relocate to Australia. He, and selected officers on his staff, departed Corregidor on March 12th by PT boat to Mindanao, where he was then airlifted in a B-17 to Australia. At a news conference following his arrival, his first act was an historic promise to the Philippine people: "I came through and I shall return." MacArthur was appointed Supreme Commander of the Southwest Pacific and led the successful march back to the Philippines. On September 2, 1945, he accepted the surrender of the Japanese on the deck of the battleship *U.S.S. Missouri*, and he then helped to build a democratic Japan while serving as Military Governor. In 1950, MacArthur became the first United Nations commander in South Korea, following the attack of that country by North Korea. When he could no longer countenance political decisions opposing his strong convictions on how the *Korean Conflict* should be fought, he was relieved of command and retired from active duty. He was invited to address Congress and received many honors, including the Military Academy's "Sylvanus Thayer Medal".

A RESPECTED LEADER COMES HOME

Jonathan M. Wainwright (Class of 1906) was the Commanding General of the Philippine Division in the North Luzon force. He was promoted to Lieutenant General, Commanding U.S. Army Forces in the Philippine Islands, and assumed his command following the emotional evacuation of Douglas MacArthur. The final Japanese assault on Bataan began on March 27th, and by April 8th all resistance on the peninsula had collapsed. The survivors withdrew to the island of Corregidor, hoping that a relief force would arrive. Corregidor, heavily bombarded, finally surrendered on May 6th. On that day Wainwright sent a message to President Roosevelt: "It is with broken heart and head bowed in sadness but not in shame, that I report to Your Excellency that I must go today to arrange terms for the surrender of the fortified islands of Manila Bay." The captured defenders of Bataan and Corregidor were imprisoned in concentration camps for the duration of the war. Wainwright was awarded the Medal of Honor for his bravery and conduct during the period March through May of 1942. His citation reads that he "*Distinguished himself by intrepid and determined leadership against greatly superior enemy forces. At the repeated risk of life above and beyond the call of duty in his position, he frequented the firing line of his troops where his presence provided the example and incentive that helped make the gallant efforts of these men possible. The final stand on beleaguered Corregidor, for which he was in an important measure personally responsible, commanded the admiration of the Nation's allies. It reflected the high morale of American arms in the face of overwhelming odds. His courage and resolution were a vitally needed inspiration to the then sorely pressed freedom-loving peoples of the world.*" President Truman presented Wainwright his Medal at the White House on September 19th, 1945. As the two talked in the Oval Office, Truman suggested a stroll in the garden because "some photographers wanted to get a picture of us together." Wainwright later wrote emotionally that "when the president stepped up and read a citation that included the words 'above and beyond the call of duty', he suddenly realized … that this was the citation for the Medal of Honor …. Nothing can supplant in my mind that afternoon in the garden of the White House." Wainwright had stood beside MacArthur at the Japanese surrender ceremony on the *U.S.S. Missouri*. He was promoted to four-star general in 1945 and commanded the Fourth Army.

A GRADUATE SAVES THE FLAG AND WRITES A POEM

An interesting human-interest story from those trying days in 1942 became public knowledge for the first time in 1945. Following the surrender of Corregidor, General MacArthur's classmate **Colonel Paul Bunker** lowered and burned the American flag, after first saving a small piece of bunting and sewing it under a patch on his uniform. As he lay sick in a hospital at Panay, he swore Colonel Delbert Ansmus to secrecy, and gave him one-half of the bunting with instructions to deliver it to the Secretary of War after the war. Ansmus sewed the bunting into the hem of his shirt, and on November 11th of 1945 he presented this last flag remnant to Secretary of War Robert P. Patterson in Washington. That remnant of our American flag from Corregidor is now in the West Point Museum.

Colonel Paul Bunker (Class of 1903), who at great personal risk had saved that piece of the American flag, died on March 16, 1943, while a prisoner of war in a camp in Formosa. During the Bataan Campaign and the subsequent siege of Corregidor Island, Colonel Bunker had kept a personal diary. His entry on Easter Sunday, April the 5th of 1942, was a poem that expressed the terrible sense of despair and loneliness that must have seized all of the final defenders on Bataan and Corregidor, when no relief had come from America after four long and bloody months of fighting. The poem was written by Bunker three days before Bataan fell to the Japanese. It sounds strangely reminiscent of that old popular cadet refrain, *Benny Havens, Oh!.*

BLOOD, SWEAT, AND TEARS

"Cut off from the land that bore us,
Betrayed by the land we find,
The brightest have gone before us,
The dullest are left behind.

"So stand to your glasses steady,
They're all you have left to prize,
Here's a cup to the dead already;
Hurrah for the next man who dies!

This poem was followed by a diary entry that said...

"Sentimental, but holding a grain of truth at that.
The worst of it is that we are being 'betrayed by
the land that bore us.'"

67

Wilbur

AN ARMISTICE OFFER IS CARRIED TO CASABLANCA

William H. Wilbur (Class of 1912), a colonel with the Western Task Force invading North Africa, landed at Fedala on November 8th of 1942. He was dressed for a parade with full ribbons and silver eagles on his uniform, and he had in his possession a message from General George Patton to the French commander in Casablanca calling for an immediate armistice. Wilbur spoke fluent French, having lived three years in France at St. Cyr and L'Ecole de Guerre. While exiting a landing craft his vehicle bogged down, but he commandeered another and drove to Casablanca, flying an American flag and a white flag to ensure his passage. Upon arriving in the town he delivered Patton's message to French officials, however Admiral Michelier refused to see him. Returning twenty miles through hostile fire to friendly lines, he took command of a tank platoon and personally directed an attack on an artillery battery that resulted in its capture. His citation reads: "*For conspicuous gallantry and intrepidity in action above and beyond the call of duty. Col. Wilbur prepared the plan for making contact with French commanders in Casablanca and obtaining an armistice to prevent unnecessary bloodshed. On 8 November 1942, he landed at Fedala with the leading assault waves where opposition had developed into a firm and continuous defensive line across his route of advance. Commandeering a vehicle, he was driven toward the hostile defenses under incessant fire, finally locating a French officer who accorded him passage through the forward positions. He then proceeded in total darkness through 16 miles of enemy-occupied country intermittently subjected to heavy bursts of fire, and accomplished his mission by delivering his letters to appropriate French officials in Casablanca. Returning toward his command, Col. Wilbur detected a hostile battery firing effectively on our troops. He took charge of a platoon of American tanks and personally led them in an attack and capture of the battery. From the moment of landing until the cessation of hostile resistance, Col. Wilbur's conduct was voluntary and exemplary in its coolness and daring.*"

Robert A. Getz

Craw

A "CEASE FIRE" MISSION SUCCEEDS IN FRENCH MOROCCO

Demas T. Craw (Class of 1924), a colonel in the U.S. Army Air Corps, was also cited for his bravery during the landings at Safi, Fedala, and Port Lyautey on the west coast of French Morocco. Craw landed near Port Lyautey and moved out in a jeep flying the American and French flags, and a white flag of truce. With him was an enlisted man and Major Pierpont M. Hamilton, a fluent French scholar. Their mission was to locate the French commander and arrange a "cease fire". They talked their way past a French battery commander and got to within two miles of Port Lyautey, when a machine gun suddenly raked the jeep with heavy fire. Craw was killed, and the others were captured by the French infantry patrol, but Hamilton delivered the "cease fire" message. Forty-eight hours later the French commanding general indicated his readiness to arrange a "cease fire" and released Hamilton. Heading back to the beach, Hamilton used a tank platoon leader's radio to advise General Patton of the "cease fire" just in time to prevent a massive air and sea bombardment of Casablanca. Craw's posthumous Medal of Honor citation reads: "*For conspicuous gallantry and intrepidity in action above and beyond the call of duty. On 8 November 1942, near Port Lyautey, French Morocco, Col. Craw volunteered to accompany the leading wave of assault boats to the shore and pass through the enemy lines to locate the French commander with a view to suspending hostilities. This request was first refused as being too dangerous but upon the officer's insistence that he was qualified to undertake and accomplish the mission he was allowed to go. Encountering heavy fire while in the landing boat and unable to dock in the river because of shell fire from shore batteries, Col. Craw, accompanied by 1 officer and 1 soldier, succeeded in landing on the beach at Mehdia Plage under constant low-level strafing from 3 enemy planes. Riding in a bantam truck toward French headquarters, progress of the party was hindered by fire from our own naval guns. Nearing Port Lyautey, Col. Craw was instantly killed by a sustained burst of machinegun fire at pointblank range from a concealed position near the road.*" The mission succeeded and saved many lives.

69

Johnson

ATTACKING THE GERMAN PLOESTI OIL REFINERIES

On August 1st, 1943, **Leon W. Johnson** (class of 1926), a colonel in the U.S. Army Air Corps and the commander of the 44th Bomber Group of the 9th Air Force, attacked the vital Ploesti oil refineries from air bases located in the Middle East. Colonel Johnson's Medal of Honor citation reads: "*For conspicuous gallantry in action and intrepidity at the risk of his life above and beyond the call of duty on 1 August 1943. Colonel Johnson, as commanding officer of a heavy bombardment group, led the formation of the aircraft of his organization constituting the fourth element of the mass low-level bombing attack of the 9th U.S. Air Force against the vitally important enemy target of the Ploesti oil refineries. While proceeding to the target on this 2,400-mile flight, his element became separated from the leading elements of the mass formation in maintaining the formation of the unit while avoiding dangerous cumulous cloud conditions encountered over mountainous territory. Though temporarily lost, he reestablished contact with the third element and continued on the mission with this reduced force to the prearranged point of attack, where it was discovered that the target assigned to Col. Johnson's group had been attacked and damaged by a preceding element. Though having lost the element of surprise upon which the safety and success of such a daring form of mission in heavy bombardment aircraft so strongly depended, Col. Johnson elected to carry out his planned low-level attack despite the thoroughly alerted defenses, the destructive antiaircraft fire, enemy fighter airplanes, the imminent danger of exploding delayed action bombs from the previous element, of oil fires and explosions, and of intense smoke obscuring the target. By his gallant courage, brilliant leadership, and superior flying skill, Col. Johnson so led his formation as to destroy totally the important refining plants and installations which were the object of his mission. Col. Johnson's personal contribution to the success of this historic raid, and the conspicuous gallantry in action, and intrepidity at the risk of his life above and beyond the call of duty demonstrated by him on this occasion constitute such deeds of valor and distinguished service as have during our Nation's history formed the finest traditions of our Armed Forces.*" Leon Johnson later remarked "*It was more like an artist's conception of an air battle than anything I had ever experienced. We flew through sheets of flames, and airplanes were everywhere, some of them on fire and others exploding.*" The intense heat rocked their planes, and they had to defend against German fighter planes on the return flight over Rumania and the Mediterranean Ocean. Of 178 attacking aircraft, only 92 completed the return leg to Benghazi. Planes landed in Sicily, Cyprus and Turkey. A total of 54 planes were lost and 532 airmen were either killed, taken prisoner, or were missing. The attack destroyed 42% of the German refining capacity at Ploesti.

Vance

A WOUNDED AIR-HERO SAVES HIS CREW

In the skies over France on the day before the D-Day invasion, code-named Operation OVERLORD, a seriously wounded airman performed incredible feats of bravery on June 5th of 1944 while attacking Calais. On July 26th, he died when the medical aircraft evacuating him to the United States from England disappeared somewhere between Iceland and Newfoundland. **Leon R. Vance, Jr**. (Class of 1939), a lieutenant colonel in the lead B-24 of his 8th Air Force bomber group, was awarded the Medal of Honor "*For conspicuous gallantry and intrepidity above and beyond the call of duty on 5 June 1944, when he led a Heavy Bombardment Group in an attack against defended enemy coastal positions in the vicinity of Wimereaux, France. Approaching the target, his aircraft was repeatedly hit by anti-aircraft fire which seriously crippled the ship, killed the pilot, and wounded several members of the crew, including Lieutenant Colonel Vance, whose right foot was practically severed. In spite of his injury, and with three engines lost to the flak, he led his formation over the target, bombing it successfully. After applying a tourniquet to his leg, with the aid of the radar operator, Lieutenant Colonel Vance, realizing that the ship was approaching a stall altitude with the one remaining engine failing, struggled to a semi-upright position beside the copilot and took over control of the ship. Cutting the power and feathering the last engine he put the aircraft in a glide sufficiently steep to maintain his airspeed. Gradually losing altitude, he at last reached the English coast, whereupon he ordered all members of the crew to bail out as he knew they would all safely make land. But he received a message over the intercom system which led him to believe one of the crew members was unable to jump due to injuries; so he made the decision to ditch the ship in the channel, thereby giving this man a chance for life. To add further to the danger of ditching the ship in his crippled condition, there was a 500-pound bomb hung up in the bomb bay. Unable to climb into the seat vacated by the copilot, since his foot, hanging onto his leg by a few tendons, had become lodged behind the copilot's seat, he nevertheless made a successful ditching while lying on the floor using only aileron and elevators for control and the side window of the cockpit for visual reference. On coming to rest in the water the aircraft commenced to sink rapidly with Lieutenant Colonel Vance pinned in the cockpit by the upper turret which had crashed in during the landing. As it was settling beneath the waves an explosion occurred which threw Lieutenant Colonel Vance clear of the wreckage. After clinging to a piece of floating wreckage until he could muster sufficient strength to inflate his life vest he began a search for the crew member whom he believed to be aboard. Failing to find anyone he began swimming and was found approximately 50 minutes later by an Air-Sea Rescue craft. By his extraordinary flying skill and gallant leadership, despite his grave injury, Lieutenant Colonel Vance led his formation to a successful bombing of the assigned target and returned the crew to a point where they could bail out with safety. His gallant and valorous decision to ditch the aircraft in order to give the crew member he believed to be aboard a chance for life exemplifies the highest tradition of the armed forces of the United States.*"

Castle

AN AIR BATTLE OVER THE ARDENNES FOREST

Frederick W. Castle, (Class of 1930), a brigadier general and the assistant commander of the 4th Bomber Wing, was on an air mission over Germany on 24 December, 1944, during the "Battle of the Bulge", when his bravery earned him a posthumous Medal of Honor. His citation states that "*He was air commander and leader of more than 2,000 heavy bombers in a strike against German airfields on 24 December 1944. En route to the target, the failure of one engine forced him to relinquish his place at the head of the formation. In order not to endanger friendly troops on the ground below, he refused to jettison his bombs to gain speed and maneuverability. His lagging, unescorted aircraft became the target of numerous enemy fighters, which ripped the left wing with cannon shells, set the oxygen system afire, and wounded two members of the crew. Repeated attacks started fires in two engines, leaving the Flying Fortress in imminent danger of exploding. Realizing the hopelessness of the situation, the bail out order was given. Without regard for his personal safety he gallantly remained alone at the controls to afford all other crewmembers an opportunity to escape. Still another attack exploded gasoline tanks in the right wing, and the bomber plunged earthward, carrying Gen. Castle to his death. His intrepidity and willing sacrifice of his life to save members of the crew were in keeping with the highest traditions of the military service.*"

A D-DAY ATTACK WITH FIXED BAYONETS

The land battle to retake Western Europe from German control began with airborne assaults and amphibious landings in France on 6 June 1944. Five days later Lt. Col. **Robert G. Cole** (Class of 1939), commanding the 3rd Battalion of the 501st Parachute Infantry Regiment, 101st Airborne Division, was attacking to secure the last four bridges over the Douve River near Carentan. Their seizure would permit the link up of troops in the *UTAH* and *OMAHA* beachheads. As his men advanced along a causeway that rose "*six to nine feet above marshes on either side*" and was "*devoid of cover*", they were subjected to heavy rifle, machine gun, and mortar fire, suffering heavy casualties from Germans dug in 150 yards away. Pinned down for an hour, Cole ordered his battalion to "*Fix bayonets*". He then stood up in the face of the devastating fire, and while waving his .45-caliber pistol he yelled "*Charge!*" and headed for the hedgerow. He had already moved fifty feet before his men "*who watched in stunned silence*" rose in small groups, following their leader. The bridge was taken. "*German bodies lay sprawled around the hedgerows, most of them dead from bayonet wounds.*" Dozens more were killed by sharpshooters while fleeing the wild charge. Cole received the Medal of Honor "*For gallantry and intrepidity at the risk of his own life, above and beyond the call of duty on 11 June 1944, in France. Lt. Col. Cole was personally leading his battalion in forcing the last of four bridges on the road to Carentan when his entire unit was suddenly pinned to the ground by intense and withering enemy rifle, machine-gun, mortar, and artillery fire placed upon them from well-prepared and heavily fortified positions within 150 yards of the foremost elements. After the devastating and unceasing enemy fire had for over one hour prevented any move and inflicted numerous casualties, Lt. Col. Cole, observing this almost helpless situation, courageously issued orders to assault the enemy positions with fixed bayonets. With utter disregard for his own safety and completely ignoring the enemy fire, he rose to his feet in front of his battalion and with drawn pistol shouted to his men to follow him in the assault. Catching up a fallen man's rifle and bayonet, he charged on and led the remnants of his battalion across the bullet-swept open ground and into the enemy position. His heroic and valiant action in so inspiring his men resulted in the complete establishment of our bridgehead across the Douve River. The cool fearlessness, personal bravery, and outstanding leadership displayed by Lt. Col. Cole reflect great credit upon himself and are worthy of the highest praise in the military service.*" A German sniper killed Cole at Nijmegen, while he was laying air-identification panels in front of his battalion's position.

73

ATTACKING SS TROOPS IN NUREMBERG

Michael J. Daly (ex-cadet of the Class of 1945) enlisted as a private in the infantry after resigning following his plebe year at the Military Academy. He fought in every major battle from OMAHA BEACH on D-Day to Nuremberg with the 1st and 3rd Infantry Divisions, while earning a battlefield commission and three Silver Stars. At the age of twenty he was a company commander in the 15th Infantry Regiment of the 3rd Infantry Division attacking Nuremberg in the "Colmar Pocket." The city was defended by hardened SS troops, and it took four days to root them out. While scouting a railroad bridge on the second day, a machinegun caught his company in the open. Daly charged to within 50 yards of the gun and killed the crew. As he continued to advance, his men said he was "*taking his life in his hands and we all knew it.*" He then attacked two more machinegun positions. Seizing a discarded M-1 rifle, he crawled to within ten yards and killed the gunners at point-blank range. Daly's Medal of Honor citation reads: "*Early in the morning of 18 April 1945, he led his company through the shell-battered, sniper-infested wreckage of Nuremberg, Germany. When blistering machinegun fire caught his unit in an exposed position, he ordered his men to take cover, dashed forward alone, and, as bullets whined about him, shot the 3-man gun crew with his carbine. Continuing the advance at the head of his company, he located an enemy patrol armed with rocket launchers, which threatened friendly armor. He again went forward alone, secured a vantage-point and opened fire on the Germans. Immediately he became the target for concentrated machine pistol and rocket fire, which blasted the rubble about him. Calmly, he continued to shoot at the patrol until he had killed all 6 enemy infantrymen. Continuing boldly far in front of his company, he entered a park, where as his men advanced, a German machinegun opened up on them without warning. With his carbine, he killed the gunner; and then from a completely exposed position he directed machinegun fire on the remainder of the crew until all were dead. In a final duel, he wiped out a third machinegun emplacement with rifle fire at a range of 10 yards. By fearlessly engaging in 4 single-handed fire fights with a desperate, powerfully armed enemy, Lieutenant Daly, voluntarily taking all major risks and protecting his men at every opportunity, killed 15 Germans, silenced 3 enemy machineguns and wiped out an entire enemy patrol. His heroism during the lone bitter struggle with fanatical enemy forces was an inspiration to the valiant Americans who took Nuremberg.*" Daly was badly wounded in the face the next day. He later said, "The medal is very important to me ... to ensure the memory of those who died."

THE KOREAN CONFLICT

THE BATTLE FOR HILL 174

On June 25, 1950, North Korea attacked South Korea. An immediate United Nations Security Council resolution called on North Korea to cease hostilities; to withdraw north of the 38th parallel of latitude; and requested all member nations to render assistance to South Korea. On July 2nd, lead elements of the 24th U.S. Infantry Division arrived at the port of Pusan and moved north to establish blocking positions above Taejon. On July 20th, the overwhelmed division began a 100-mile withdrawal into the Pusan Perimeter, where a stubborn defense finally blunted the enemy advance. A month long stalemate was broken on September 15th by an amphibious landing on the Korean west coast at Inchon and a breakout from the Pusan Perimeter by the 1st Cavalry Division. The division led the attack north, crossing the thirty-eighth parallel on October 9th against strong resistance. Near Kaesong, 1st Lieutenant **Samuel S. Coursen** (Class of 1949), a platoon leader in Company C, 5th Cavalry Regiment, attacked Hill 174 on October 12th. As his platoon moved down the hill's reverse slope, they were subjected to *"heavy fire from a well-concealed strong point."* He continued to attack through the fog. As the enemy fire increased, one soldier, seeking cover, mistakenly dived into an enemy occupied bunker. *"Nearly a dozen North Korean soldiers fell on the hapless American. Coursen heard the man's screams for help. Without a second of hesitation, he plunged into the emplacement. He fought like a cornered tiger ... used his carbine as a club."* When he was later found, he *"lay dead on top of one of the enemy soldiers, shot in the back...."* Coursen's citation reads: *"Lieutenant Coursen distinguished himself by conspicuous gallantry and intrepidity above and beyond the call of duty in action. While Company C was attacking Hill 174 under heavy enemy small-arms fire, his platoon received enemy fire from close range. The platoon returned the fire and continued to advance. During this phase one of his men moved into a well-camouflaged emplacement, which was thought to be unoccupied, and was wounded by the enemy who were hidden within the emplacement. Seeing the soldier in difficulty he rushed to the man's aid and, without regard for his personal safety, engaged the enemy in hand-to-hand combat in an effort to protect his wounded comrade until he himself was killed. When his body was recovered after the battle 7 enemy dead were found in the emplacement. As the result of 1st Lt. Coursen's violent struggle several of the enemies' heads had been crushed with his rifle. His aggressive and intrepid actions saved the life of the wounded man, eliminated the main position of the enemy roadblock, and greatly inspired the men in his command. 1st Lt. Coursen's extraordinary heroism and intrepidity reflect the highest credit on himself and are in keeping with the honored traditions of the military service."*

THE DEFENSE OF PORK CHOP HILL

Talks between North Korea, the Chinese, and the United Nations initially began in the summer of 1951 at Kaesong, and then moved to Panmunjom. However, the fighting continued right up to the signing of an armistice at Panmunjom on 27 July 1953. In early July, an American position on Pork Chop Hill near Sokkogae was aggressively attacked in the night by the Chinese *"in a driving summer rainstorm."* 1st Lieutenant **Richard T. Shea** (Class of 1952), Company A, 17th Infantry Regiment, 7th Infantry Division was awarded the Medal of Honor for his heroism from the 6th to the 8th of July. Chinese attacks had managed to seize a trench line just before dawn on the 6th. Discovered by Shea, he charged with his .45-caliber pistol and killed four or five of the enemy. Then using his trench knife he killed two more and drove the remainder away. The next afternoon, already wounded, he attacked a machinegun a few yards away with grenades. He then stood up, and with walking-fire from his carbine killed the three-man crew. His company commander said: *"He was almost a one man assault. He was again wounded, but continued with a courage I have never seen displayed by any man. He continued fighting and gaining terrain."* Shea's citation reads: *"1st Lieutenant Shea, executive officer, Company A, distinguished himself by conspicuous gallantry and indomitable courage above and beyond the call of duty in action against the enemy. On the night of 6 July, he was supervising the reinforcement of defensive positions when the enemy attacked with great numerical superiority. Voluntarily proceeding to the area most threatened, he organized and led a counterattack and, in the bitter fighting that ensued, closed with and killed 2 hostile soldiers with his trench knife. Calmly moving among the men, checking positions, steadying and urging the troops to hold firm, he fought side by side with them throughout the night. Despite heavy losses, the hostile force pressed the assault with determination, and at dawn made an all-out attempt to overrun friendly elements. Charging forward to meet the challenge, 1st Lt. Shea and his gallant men drove back the hostile troops. Elements of Company G joined the defense on the afternoon of 7 July, having lost key personnel through casualties. Immediately integrating these troops into his unit, 1st Lt. Shea rallied a group of 20 men and again charged the enemy. Although wounded in this action, he refused evacuation and continued to lead the counterattack. When the assaulting element was pinned down by heavy machinegun fire, he personally rushed the emplacement and, firing his carbine and lobbing grenades with deadly accuracy, neutralized the weapon and killed 3 of the enemy. With forceful leadership and by his heroic example, 1st Lt. Shea coordinated and directed a holding action throughout the night and the following morning. On 8 July, the enemy attacked again. Despite additional wounds, he launched a determined counterattack and was last seen in close hand-to-hand combat with the enemy. 1st Lt. Shea's inspirational leadership and unflinching courage set an illustrious example of valor to the men of his regiment, reflecting lasting glory upon himself and upholding the noble traditions of the military service."*

THE VIETNAM CONFLICT

It started with the dispatch in 1962 of advisors to assist the South Vietnamese army in its struggle against Viet Cong guerillas supported by the North Vietnamese, and it lasted until 1975. This was the "cold war" period - the "Free World versus Communism" - and the expectation of a "domino effect" in Southeast Asia, should South Vietnam fall, motivated America's military commitment. Unfortunately, the conflict was fought in gradually escalating increments of force, and, as the years rolled by, the intensity of the fighting reached levels that had not been thought possible in the earlier years. By 1967, over 500,000 troops were fighting in-country; billions of dollars were being spent; politicians were micro-managing strategy, tactics, and basic military decisions such as target selection; and draft-age youths were dominating the media news with street demonstrations. Americans were traveling to Hanoi and European cities giving aid and psychological comfort to the North Vietnamese enemy. Politicians lost their nerve; and a president decided not to run for re-election. Through it all, no flag officers or senior administration political appointees chose to resign and to publicly protest the way in which the conflict was being fought. Few seemed to appreciate or anticipate during those 12 long years either the short term or long term effects of their policy decisions. Only now are a few of those responsible decision-makers stepping forward to air their mistakes, but none spoke out publicly 30 years ago. Many of the long-term effects of the *Vietnam Conflict* are still with us. The "draft" is gone and no longer do we have a "citizen army" with the wide national base of support of prior years. No longer do politicians feel the constituent pressure of strong citizen interest in sound political decisions being made when our troops are committed in "harm's way". We now have a "volunteer army", and having bought into that concept as an aftermath of Vietnam, the public now goes about its daily business mostly oblivious to military matters. An irrational national aversion to incur war casualties has also carried over from Vietnam. This aversion interferes even today with the making of important political and military decisions to defend loosely defined "national interests", because those decisions might result in unacceptable casualties. The media and the public focus on friendly casualty lists is still with us. We have not overcome these and other serious after-effects of the *Vietnam Conflict*. In spite of the final result, however, the *Vietnam Conflict* was fought by a highly dedicated and professional army, and included many heroes on the ground and in the air. Their conduct was even more remarkable given the continuous depressing nightly news from the home front. No, the outcome of the *Vietnam Conflict* was not their fault. There were seven Medal of Honor recipients in the *Vietnam Conflict* who attended the Military Academy.

DONLON

78

THE DEFENSE OF CAMP NAM DONG

Captain **Roger Hugh C. Donlon** (ex-cadet of the Class of 1959), commanding a Special Forces team in the Central Highlands near Khe Sanh and the Laos border, received the very first Medal of Honor in Vietnam for his bravery on 17 December 1964. His force of 300 men was mostly Vietnamese and Montagnards. He was cited "For conspicuous gallantry and intrepidity at the risk of his life above and beyond the call of duty while defending a U.S. military installation against a fierce attack by hostile forces. Capt. Donlon was serving as the commanding officer of the U.S. Army Special Forces Detachment A-726 at Camp Nam Dong when a reinforced Viet Cong battalion suddenly launched a full-scale, predawn attack on the camp. During the violent battle that ensued, lasting 5 hours and resulting in heavy casualties on both sides, Capt. Donlon directed the defense operations in the midst of an enemy barrage of mortar shells, falling grenades, and extremely heavy gunfire. Upon the initial onslaught, he swiftly marshalled his forces and ordered the removal of the needed ammunition from a blazing building. He then dashed through a hail of small arms and exploding hand grenades to abort a breach of the main gate. En route to this position he detected an enemy demolition team of 3 in the proximity of the main gate and quickly annihilated them. Although exposed to the intense grenade attack, he then succeeded in reaching a 60mm mortar position despite sustaining a severe stomach wound as he was within 5 yards of the gunpit. When he discovered that most of the men in this gunpit were also wounded, he completely disregarded his injury, directed their withdrawal to a location 30 meters away, and again risked his life by remaining behind and covering the movement with the utmost effectiveness. Noticing that his team sergeant was unable to evacuate the gunpit, he crawled toward him and, while dragging the fallen soldier out of the gunpit, an enemy mortar exploded and inflicted a wound in Capt. Donlon's left shoulder. Although suffering from multiple wounds, he carried the abandoned 60mm mortar to a new location 30 meters away where he found 3 wounded defenders. After administering first aid and encouragement to these men, he left the weapon with them, headed toward another position, and retrieved a 57mm recoilless rifle. Then with great courage and coolness under fire, he returned to the abandoned gunpit, evacuated ammunition for the two weapons, and while crawling and dragging the urgently needed ammunition, received a third wound on his leg by an enemy hand grenade. Despite his critical physical condition, he again crawled 175 meters to an 81mm mortar position and directed firing operations which protected the seriously threatened east sector of the camp. He then moved to an eastern 60mm mortar position, set it up for defensive operations, and turned it over to 2 defenders with minor wounds. Without hesitation, he left this sheltered position, and moved from position to position around the beleaguered perimeter while hurling hand grenades at the enemy and inspiring his men to superhuman effort. As he bravely continued to move around the perimeter, a mortar shell exploded, wounding him in the face and body. As the long awaited daylight brought defeat to the enemy forces and their retreat back to the jungle leaving 54 of their dead, many weapons, and grenades, Capt. Donlon immediately reorganized his defenses and administered first aid to the wounded. His dynamic leadership, fortitude, and valiant efforts inspired not only the American personnel but the friendly Vietnamese defenders as well and resulted in the successful defense of the camp. Capt. Donlon's extraordinary heroism, at the risk of his life above and beyond the call of duty are in the highest traditions of the U.S. Army and reflect great credit upon himself and the Armed Forces of his country." When a mortar round landed in his face "Donlon remembered screaming as he took the brunt of the explosion. 'I am going to die, I thought. The screaming ... was the wail of death." He tended Montagnarde wounds using his T-shirt and a sock as tourniquets. From the jungle a voice called in English and Vietnamese, "Lay down your weapons! We are going to annihilate your camp! You will all be killed!" But they held out and killed 50 Viet Cong of an estimated 800.

REASONER

A MARINE PATROL NEAR DANANG

Frank S. Reasoner (Class of 1962) entered the Marine Corps after graduation from the Military Academy, where he had won the boxing Brigade Championship in four different weight classes and also excelled in baseball and wrestling. He had served three years in the Marine Corps before entering the Academy, and in 1965 he was a 1st lieutenant in Company A, 3rd Reconnaissance Battalion, 3rd Marine Division, located near Danang. "Reasoner was well-respected and loved by his marines. He in turn, loved and respected them." On 12 July, he was leading a routine patrol on a reconnaissance mission in an area that *"was a flat, dangerous land, spotted with tree lines and hedgerows. It was perfect country for an ambush."* The patrol's mission *"was a routine sweep of a suspected VC area ... to deter any VC activity aimed at the airbase at Danang."* His unit was suddenly *"viciously attacked by an estimated fifty to one hundred Viet Cong."* Reasoner's citation reads: *"For conspicuous gallantry and intrepidity in action at the risk of his life above and beyond the call of duty. The reconnaissance patrol led by 1st Lt. Reasoner had deeply penetrated heavily controlled enemy territory when it came under extremely heavy fire from an estimated 50 to 100 Viet Cong insurgents. Accompanying the advance party and the point that consisted of 5 men, he immediately deployed his men for an assault after the Viet Cong had opened fire from numerous concealed positions. Boldly shouting encouragement, and virtually isolated from the main body, he organized a base of fire for an assault on the enemy positions. The slashing fury of the Viet Cong machinegun and automatic weapons fire made it impossible for the main body to move forward. Repeatedly exposing himself to the devastating attack he skillfully provided covering fire, killing at least 2 Viet Cong and effectively silencing an automatic weapons position in a valiant attempt to effect evacuation of a wounded man. As casualties began to mount his radio operator was wounded and 1st Lt. Reasoner immediately moved to his side and tended his wounds. When the radio operator was hit a second time while attempting to reach a covered position, 1st Lt. Reasoner courageously running to his aid through the grazing machinegun fire fell mortally wounded. His indomitable fighting spirit, valiant leadership and unflinching devotion to duty provided the inspiration that was to enable the patrol to complete its mission without further casualties. In the face of almost certain death he gallantly gave his life in the service of his country. His actions upheld the highest traditions of the Marine Corps and the U.S. Naval Service.* Having been an enlisted marine prior to entering the Military Academy, Reasoner felt a special obligation to always care and tend to his troops. When his radio operator was hit, he comforted him by saying *"Take it easy son. We'll get you out of here."* Three hours after leaving his base camp, Reasoner's body was returned in a helicopter. "A young corporal sobbed uncontrollably as he jumped from the chopper, 'My skipper's dead. He should be covered up. Will someone get a blanket?'" Navy Secretary Paul H. Nitze, who presented the Medal of Honor to his widow and son, said, *"Lieutenant Reasoner's complete disregard for his own welfare will long serve as an inspiring example to others."*

GARDNER

Robert A. Getz 97 ©

ASSAULTING BUNKER FORTIFICATIONS NEAR MY CANH

1st Lieutenant **James A. Gardner** (ex-cadet of the Class of 1965), Headquarters and Headquarters Company, 1st Battalion (Airborne), 327th Infantry, 1st Brigade, 101st Airborne Division, *"was ordered to take his platoon around behind My Canh and destroy the enemy from behind."* On February 7, 1966, Gardner was leading a relief platoon attacking to prevent the destruction of a pinned down company. His platoon was also immediately pinned down *"by heavy rifle fire from a series of supportive bunkers."* Single handedly Gardner attacked and eliminated several bunkers, before falling dead as he destroyed a final bunker with his dying effort. It was his twenty-third birthday. His citation reads: *"For conspicuous gallantry and intrepidity in action at the risk of his life above and beyond the call of duty. 1st Lt. Gardner's platoon was advancing to relieve a company of the 1st Battalion that had been pinned down for several hours by a numerically superior enemy force in the village of My Canh, Vietnam. The enemy occupied a series of strongly fortified bunker positions, which were mutually supporting and expertly concealed. Approaches to the position were well covered by an integrated pattern of fire including automatic weapons, machineguns and mortars. Air strikes and artillery placed on the fortifications had little effect. 1st Lt. Gardner's platoon was to relieve the friendly company by encircling and destroying the enemy force. Even as it moved to begin the attack, the platoon was under heavy enemy fire. During the attack, the enemy fire intensified. Leading the assault and disregarding his own safety, 1st Lt. Gardner charged through a withering hail of fire across an open rice paddy. On reaching the first bunker he destroyed it with a grenade and without hesitation dashed to the second bunker and eliminated it by tossing a grenade inside. Then, crawling swiftly along the dike of a rice paddy, he reached the third bunker. Before he could arm a grenade, the enemy gunner leaped forth, firing at him. 1st Lt. Gardner instantly returned the fire and killed the enemy gunner at a distance of 6 feet. Following the seizure of the main enemy position, he reorganized the platoon to continue the attack. Advancing to the new assault position, the platoon was pinned down by an enemy machinegun emplaced in a fortified bunker. 1st Lt. Gardner immediately collected several grenades and charged the enemy position, firing his rifle he advanced to neutralize the defender. He dropped a grenade into the bunker and vaulted beyond. As the bunker blew up, he came under fire again. Rolling into a ditch to gain cover, he moved toward the new source of fire. Nearing the position, he leaped from the ditch and advanced with a grenade in one hand and firing his rifle with the other. He was gravely wounded just before he reached the bunker, but with a last valiant effort he staggered forward and destroyed the bunker, and its defenders with a grenade. Although he fell dead on the rim of the bunker, his extraordinary actions so inspired the men of his platoon that they resumed the attack and completely routed the enemy. 1st Lt. Gardner's conspicuous gallantry were in the highest traditions of the U.S. Army."* Gardner's parents were presented with his Medal of Honor.

FOLEY

84

A JUNGLE ASSAULT RELIEVES A BESIEGED COMPANY

Captain **Robert F. Foley** (Class of 1963), Company A, 2nd Battalion, 27th Infantry, 25th Division, had the mission of rescuing a company pinned down by the 9th Viet Cong Division in Tay Ninh Province near Quan Dau Tieng on November 5, 1966. Foley, "*in spite of several wounds, destroyed three enemy machineguns, helped several wounded members of his company to safety, and continued to lead his men in the fight.*" His Medal of Honor citation reads: "*For conspicuous gallantry and intrepidity in action at the risk of his life above and beyond the call of duty. Capt. Foley's company was ordered to extricate another company of the battalio. Moving through the dense jungle to aid the besieged unit, Company A encountered a strong enemy force occupying well concealed, defensive positions, and the company's leading element quickly sustained several casualties. Capt. Foley immediately ran forward to the scene of the most intense action to direct the company's efforts. Deploying one platoon on the flank, he led the other two platoons in an attack on the enemy in the face of intense fire. During this action both radio operators accompanying him were wounded. At grave risk to himself he defied the enemy's murderous fire, and helped the wounded operators to a position where they could receive medical care. As he moved forward again 1 of his machinegun crews was wounded. Seizing the weapon, he charged forward firing the machinegun, shouting orders and rallying his men, thus maintaining the momentum of the attack. Under increasingly heavy enemy fire he ordered his assistant to take cover and, alone, Capt. Foley continued to advance firing the machinegun until the wounded had been evacuated and the attack in this area could be resumed. When movement on the other flank was halted by the enemy's fanatical defense, Capt. Foley moved to personally direct this critical phase of the battle. Leading the renewed effort he was blown off his feet and wounded by an enemy grenade. Despite his painful wounds, he refused medical aid and persevered in the forefront of the attack on the enemy redoubt. He led the assault on several enemy gun emplacements and, singlehandedly, destroyed 3 such positions. His outstanding personal leadership under intense enemy fire during the fierce battle which lasted for several hours, inspired his men to heroic efforts and was instrumental in the ultimate success of the operation. Capt. Foley's magnificent courage, selfless concern for his men and professional skill reflect the utmost credit upon himself and the U.S. Army.*" Foley received his Medal at a White House ceremony on 1 May 1968.

BUCHA

Robert A. Getz '90

A NIGHT MEETING ENGAGEMENT IN BINH DUONG PROVINCE

Captain **Paul W. Bucha** (Class of 1965), Company D, 3rd Battalion, 187th Infantry, 3rd Brigade, 101st Airborne Division, was on an offensive that began on March 16, 1968. After fighting for three days and destroying an enemy base camp, they were settling in for the night of March 18th, when they encountered a North Vietnamese battalion that was also preparing for the night. The company was pinned down with a "*veritable hail of heavy automatic-weapons fire, rocket propelled grenades (RPG's), claymore mines, and small arms fire.*" Bucha earned the Medal of Honor that night. He recalls, "*It was just getting dark....They hit us with everything they had. We tried to hold on until daylight.*" His citation reads: "*For conspicuous gallantry and intrepidity in action at the risk of his life above and beyond the call of duty. Capt. Bucha distinguished himself while serving as commanding officer, Company D, on a reconnaissance-in-force against enemy forces near Phouc Vinh. The company was inserted by helicopter into the suspected enemy stronghold to locate and destroy the enemy. During this period Capt. Bucha aggressively and courageously led his men in the destruction of enemy fortifications and base areas and eliminated scattered resistance impeding the advance of the company. On 18 March while advancing to contact, the lead elements of the company became engaged by the heavy automatic weapon, heavy machinegun, rocket-propelled grenade, claymore mine and small arms fire of an estimated battalion-size force. Capt. Bucha, with complete disregard for his safety, moved to the threatened area to direct the defense and ordered reinforcements to the aid of the lead element. Seeing that his men were pinned down by heavy machinegun fire from a concealed bunker located some 40 meters to the front of the positions, Capt. Bucha crawled through the hail of fire to singlehandedly destroy the bunker with grenades. During this heroic action Capt. Bucha received a painful shrapnel wound. Returning to the perimeter, he observed that his unit could not hold its positions and repel the human wave assaults launched by the determined enemy. Capt. Bucha ordered the withdrawal of the unit elements and covered the withdrawal to positions of a company perimeter from which he could direct fire upon the charging enemy. When 1 friendly element retrieving casualties was ambushed and cut off from the perimeter, Capt. Bucha ordered them to feign death and he directed artillery fire around them. During the night Capt. Bucha moved throughout the position, distributing ammunition, providing encouragement and insuring the integrity of the defense. He directed artillery, helicopter gunship and Air Force gunship fire on the enemy strong points and attacking forces, marking the positions with smoke-grenades. Using flashlights in complete view of enemy snipers, he directed the medical evacuation of three air-ambulance loads of seriously wounded personnel and the helicopter supply of his company. At daybreak Capt. Bucha led a rescue party to recover the dead and wounded members of the ambushed element. During the period of intensive combat, Capt. Bucha, by his extraordinary heroism, inspirational example, outstanding leadership and professional competence, led his company in the decimation of a superior enemy force which left 156 dead on the battlefield. His bravery and gallantry at the risk of his life are in the highest traditions of the military service. Capt. Bucha has reflected great credit on himself, his unit, and the U.S. Army.* In accepting the Medal, Bucha said that he holds the Medal on behalf of his company. He said, "I am as proud of them as I am of the Medal. I feel I accepted the award more for them than myself."

JONES

Robert A. Getz 99©

AN AIRMAN HELPS SAVE A DOWNED PILOT

Colonel **William A. Jones, III** (Class of 1945), U.S. Air Force, 602nd Special Operations Squadron, Nakon Phanom Royal Thai Air Force Base, Thailand, was awarded the Medal of Honor for his heroism in attempting to rescue a downed U.S. pilot on 1 September, 1968, near Dong Hoi, North Vietnam. His citation reads: *"For conspicuous gallantry and intrepidity in action at the risk of his life above and beyond the call of duty. Col. Jones distinguished himself as the pilot of an A-1H Skyraider aircraft near Dong Hoi, North Vietnam. On that day, as the on-scene commander in the attempted rescue of a downed U.S. pilot, Col. Jones' aircraft was repeatedly hit by heavy and accurate antiaircraft fire. On one of his low passes, Col. Jones felt an explosion beneath his aircraft and his cockpit rapidly filled with smoke. With complete disregard of the possibility that his aircraft might still be burning, he unhesitatingly continued his search for the downed pilot. On this pass, he sighted the survivor and a multiple-barrel gun position firing at him from near the top of a karst formation. He could not attack the gun position on that pass for fear he would endanger the downed pilot. Leaving himself exposed to the gun position, Col. Jones attacked the position with cannon and rocket fire on 2 successive passes. On his second pass, the aircraft was hit with multiple rounds of automatic weapons fire. One round impacted the Yankee Extraction System rocket mounted directly behind the headrest, igniting the rocket. His aircraft was observed to burst into flames in the center fuselage section, with flames engulfing the cockpit area. He pulled the extraction handle, jettisoning the canopy. The influx of fresh air made the fire burn with greater intensity for a few moments, but since the rocket motor had all ready burned, the extraction system did not pull Col. Jones from the aircraft. Despite searing pains from severe burns sustained on his arms, hands, neck, shoulders and face, Col. Jones pulled his aircraft into a climb and attempted to transmit the location of the downed pilot and the enemy gun position to the other aircraft in the area. His calls were blocked by other aircraft transmissions repeatedly directing him to bail out and within seconds his transmitters were disabled and he could receive only 1 channel. Completely disregarding his injuries, he elected to fly his crippled aircraft back to his base and pass on essential information for the rescue rather than bail out. Col. Jones successfully landed his heavily damaged aircraft and passed the information to a debriefing officer while on the operating table. As a result of his heroic actions and complete disregard for his personal safety, the downed pilot was rescued later in the day. Col. Jones' profound concern for his fellow man at the risk of his life, above and beyond the call of duty, are in keeping with the highest traditions of the U.S. Air Force and reflect great credit upon himself and the Armed Forces of his country."*

LUCAS

Robert A. Getz 99

A BATTALION COMMANDER FIGHTS TO SAVE HIS TROOPS

Lieutenant Colonel **Andre Cavaro Lucas** (Class of 1954), 2nd Battalion, 506th Infantry, 101st Airborne Division, was the commander of Fire Support Base "Ripcord" during the period 1 to 23 July, 1970, when his heroism earned him the posthumous award of the Medal of Honor. Lucas was an outstanding infantry officer whose tours of duty included serving as a tactical officer at the Military Academy; troop assignments with the 82nd Airborne Division; and commander of an infantry battalion in Germany before taking command of a second battalion in combat in Vietnam. In the short year that Lucas was in Vietnam, his bravery was recognized with two Silver Stars, a Bronze Star Medal for valor, and the posthumous award of the Medal of Honor. His other decorations awarded during a too short career included the Legion of Merit, the Air Medal, and two Commendation Medals. Andre Lucas' citation for the Medal of Honor reads: *"Lt. Col. Lucas distinguished himself by extraordinary heroism while serving as the commanding officer of the 2nd Battalion. Although the fire base was constantly subjected to heavy attacks by a numerically superior enemy force throughout this period, Lt. Col. Lucas, forsaking his own safety, performed numerous acts of extraordinary valor in directing the defense of the allied position. On 1 occasion, he flew in a helicopter at treetop level above an entrenched enemy directing the fire of 1 of his companies for over 3 hours. Even though his helicopter was heavily damaged by enemy fire, he remained in an exposed position until the company expended its supply of grenades. He then transferred to another helicopter, dropped critically needed grenades to the troops, and resumed his perilous mission of directing fire on the enemy. These courageous actions by Lt. Col. Lucas prevented the company from being encircled and destroyed by a larger enemy force. On another occasion, Lt. Col. Lucas attempted to rescue a crewman trapped in a burning helicopter. As the flames in the aircraft spread, and enemy fire became intense, Lt. Col. Lucas ordered all members of the rescue party to safety. Then, at great personal risk, he continued the rescue effort amid concentrated enemy mortar fire, intense heat, and exploding ammunition until the aircraft was completely engulfed in flames. Lt. Col. Lucas was mortally wounded while directing the successful withdrawal of his battalion from the fire base. His actions throughout this extended period inspired his men to heroic efforts, and were instrumental in saving the lives of many of his fellow soldiers while inflicting heavy casualties on the enemy. Lt. Col. Lucas' conspicuous gallantry and intrepidity in action, at the cost of his own life, were in keeping with the highest traditions of the military service and reflect great credit on him, his unit and the U.S. Army."*

BIBLIOGRAPHY

Ambrose, Stephen E. *Duty, Honor, Country, A History of West Point*. Baltimore, MD: Johns Hopkins Press. 1966.

Ambrose, Stephen E. *D-Day June 6th, 1944: Climactic Battle of World War II*. New York: Simon & Schuster. 1994.

Association of Graduates. *Assembly (Spring 1970 and July 1954 issues)*. West Point, NY.

Association of Graduates. *Register of Graduates*. West Point, NY: 1974.

Association of Graduates. *Register of Graduates*. West Point, NY: 1990.

Association of Graduates. *Register of Graduates*. West Point, NY: 1994.

Axelrod, Alan. *Chronicle of the Indian Wars*. New York: Prentice Hall. 1993.

Brown, Dee. *Bury My Heart at Wounded Knee*. Canada: Holt, Rinehart & Winston of Canada. 1970.

Capps, Benjamin. *The Old West, The Indians*. New York: Time Life. 1973.

Castle. *Battles and Leaders of the Civil War, Vol. I thru IV*. Secaucus, NJ: Based on "*The Century*" magazine series, November 1884-November 1887.

Catton, Bruce. *The Army of the Potomac*. New York: Doubleday & Company, Inc. 1952.

Catton, Bruce. *Terrible Swift Sword*. New York: Doubleday & Company, Inc. 1963.

Center of Military History, U.S. Army. *American Armies and Battlefields in Europe*. Washington D.C. 1992.

Clodfelter, Michael. *Warfare and Armed Conflicts. Vol II 1900-1991*. Jefferson, NC: McFarland & Company, Inc. 1992.

Correspondence Relating to the War with Spain, including the Insurrection in the Philippine Islands And the China Relief Expedition April 15, 1898 to July 30, 1902. Volume 2. Washington DC. Government Printing Office. 1902.

Davis, Burke. *To Appomattox*. New York: Rinehart & Company, Inc. 1959.

Dillon, Richard H. *North American Indian Wars*. New York: Gallery Books. 1983.

Dupuy, Ernest R. *Men of West Point*. New York: William Sloane Associates. 1951.

Editors Boston Publishing Co. *Above and Beyond*. Boston, Mass. 1985.

Faust, Karl Irving. *Campaigning in the Philippines*. New York: Arno Press & New York Times. 1970.

Foote, Shelby. *The Civil War, A Narrative, Fredericksburg to Meridian*. New York: Random House. 1963.

Garrison, Webb. *A Treasury of Civil War Tales*. New York: Rutledge Hill Press. 1988.

Greeley, Horace. *The American Conflict, A History of the Great Rebellion in the U.S.A., Vol. I*. Chicago: O.D. Case & Co. 1865.

Grinnel, George. *The Fighting Cheyenne*. New York: Charles Scribner Sons. 1915.

Highland House II. *United States of America's Congressional Medal of Honor Recipients*. Columbia Heights, MN: Highland Publishers. 1994.

Lang, George; Collins, Raymond; and White, Gerard F. *Medal of Honor Recipients, 1863-1991*, 2 Volumes. New York: Facts on File, Inc.. 1995.

Lawson, Don. *The United States in the Spanish-American War*. New York: Abelard-Schuman. 1976.

Marshall, S.L.A. *Crimsoned Prairie*. New York: Charles Scribner Sons. 1972.

Moses, Edward; and Getz, Robert. *West Point, The Making of Leaders, An Historical Sketchbook. Revised Edition*. Alexandria, VA. Moses and Getz Publishers. 1995.

Murphy, Edward F. *Vietnam Medal of Honor Heroes*. New York: Random House, Inc. 1987.

Murphy, Edward F. *Heroes of World War II*. Novato, CA: Presidio Press. 1990.

Murphy, Edward F. *Korean War Heroes*. Novato, CA: Presidio Press. 1972.

Musicant, Ivan. *Empire By Default, The Spanish-American War and the Dawn of the American Century*. New York: Henry Holt and Company. 1998.

O'Toole, G.J.A. *The Spanish-American War, An American Epic 1898*. New York: W.W. Norton & Co. 1986.

Readers Digest. *Through Indian Eyes*. New York: Readers Digest Association. 1995.

Ridpath, John C. *History of the United States*. Chicago: C.B. Beach & Co. 1877.

Roberts, David. *Once They Moved Like the Wind*. New York: Simon & Shuster. 1993.

Sommers, Richard J. *Richmond Redeemed*. New York: Doubleday & Company, Inc. 1981.

Sonnicksen, C.L. *The Mescalero Apaches*. Norman, OK: University of Oklahoma Press. 1966.

Stands in Timber, John and Liberty, Margot. *Cheyenne Memories*. New Haven, CN: Yale University Press. 1967.

Sweeney, Edwin R. *Cochise, Chiricahua Apache Chief*. Norman, OK: University of Oklahoma Press. 1991.

Symonds, Craig L. *A Battlefield Atlas of the Civil War*. Annapolis, MD: Nautical & Aviation Publishing Company of America. 1983.

Tate, Allen. *Stonewall Jackson. The Good Soldier*. New York: Minton, Balch & Company. 1928.

Tullai, Martin D. *Marching on Full Ration of Humor*. The Washington Times. May 5, 1995.

USMA. *Bugle Notes 1992-1996*. West Point, NY: 1992.

USMA. *Medal of Honor Memorial Booklet*. West Point, NY: 1963.

Utley, Robert M. *Frontier Regulars, The United States Army and the Indian 1866-1890*. New York: MacMillan Publishing Co., Inc. 1973.

Utley, Robert M. and Washburn, Wilcomb E.. *The Indian Wars*. New York: American Heritage. 1977.

Walsh, John. *The Philippine Insurrection 1899-1902*. New York: Franklin Watts, Inc. 1925.

APPENDIX 1

THE UNITED STATES MILITARY ACADEMY
MEDAL OF HONOR RECIPIENTS
(listed by Conflict first, then by Association of Graduates #, and then by Class)

CONFLICT	NAME	AOG #	CLASS
Civil War	John Cleveland Robinson	**	1839
Civil War	John Porter Hatch	1247	1845
Civil War	Orlando Bolivar Willcox	1338	1847
Civil War	Absalom Baird	1415	1849
Civil War	Rufus Saxton, Jr.	1424	1849
Civil War	Eugene Asa Carr	1468	1850
Civil War	Charles H. Tompkins	**	1851
Civil War	David Sloan Stanley	1544	1852
Civil War	John McAllister Schofield	1585	1853
Civil War	Oliver Otis Howard	1634	1854
Civil War	Oliver Duff Greene	1656	1854
Civil War	Zenas Randall Bliss	1671	1854
Civil War	Alexander Stewart Webb	1689	1855
Civil War	Abraham Kerns Arnold	1845	1858
Civil War	Horace Porter	1849	1860
Civil War	John Moulder Wilson	1858	1860
Civil War	Henry Algernon Dupont	1888	1861(May)
Civil War	Adelbert Ames	1892	1861(May)
Civil War	Samuel Nicoll Benjamin	1899	1861(May)
Civil War	Guy Vernor Henry	1914	1861(May)
Civil War	Eugene Beauharnais Beaumont	1919	1861(May)
Civil War	George Lewis Gillespie, Jr.	1968	1862
Civil War	William Henry Harrison Benyaurd	2000	1863
Civil War	William Sully Beebe	2009	1863

Civil War	John Gregory Bourke (Enlisted)	2283	1869
Indian Campaigns	Edward Settle Godfrey	2208	1867
Indian Campaigns	William Preble Hall	2246	1868
Indian Campaigns	Edward John McClernand	2347	1870
Indian Campaigns	Robert Goldthwaite Carter	2349	1870
Indian Campaigns	John Brown Kerr	2362	1870
Indian Campaigns	Charles Albert Varnum	2427	1872
Indian Campaigns	Frank West	2428	1872
Indian Campaigns	William Harding Carter	2502	1873
Indian Campaigns	Marion Perry Maus	2545	1874
Indian Campaigns	Oscar Fitzalan Long	2614	1876
Indian Campaigns	Ernest Albert Garlington	2622	1876
Indian Campaigns	John Chowning Gresham	2626	1876
Indian Campaigns	Wilbur Elliott Wilder	2672	1877
Indian Campaigns	Robert Temple Emmet	2693	1877
Indian Campaigns	Matthias Walter Day	2710	1877
Indian Campaigns	Thomas Cruse	2785	1879
Indian Campaigns	Lloyd Milton Brett	2793	1879
Indian Campaigns	George Horace Morgan	2858	1880
Indian Campaigns	George Ritter Burnett	2876	1880
Indian Campaigns	Powhatan Henry Clarke	3057	1884
Indian Campaigns	Robert Lee Howze	3260	1888
China Relief Exp.	Louis Bowen Lawton	3533	1893
China Relief Exp.	Calvin Pearl Titus (Enlisted)	4380	1905
Cuba Campaign	Albert Leopold Mills	2796	1879
Cuba Campaign	John Wilkinson Heard	3001	1883
Cuba Campaign	Charles DuVall Roberts	3749	1897
Cuba Campaign	Ira Clinton Welborn	3847	1898
Philippine Insurrection	William Edward Birkhimer	2330	1870
Philippine Insurrection	James Parker	2623	1873
Philippine Insurrection	James Franklin Bell	2754	1878

Philippine Insurrection	Hugh Jocelyn McGrath	2850	1880
Philippine Insurrection	William Hampden Sage	2952	1882
Philippine Insurrection	*John Alexander Logan, Jr.*	**	1887
Philippine Insurrection	Louis Joseph Van Schaick	**	1900
Moro Expedition	Arthur Harrison Wilson	4331	1904
Moro Expedition	John Thomas Kennedy	4684	1908
Vera Cruz	Eli Thompson Fryer	**	1901
World War I	*Emory Jenison Pike*	4066	1901
World War II	Douglas MacArthur	4122	1903
World War II	Jonathan Mayhew Wainwright	4477	1906
World War II	William Hale Wilbur	5042	1912
World War II	*Demas Thurlow Craw*	*7590	1924
World War II	Leon William Johnson	*7930	1926
World War II	*Frederick Walker Castle*	*8792	1930
World War II	*Robert George Cole*	11630	1939
World War II	*Leon Robert Vance, Jr.*	*11652	1939
World War II	*Alexander Ramsey Nininger, Jr.*	12317	1941
World War II	Michael Joseph Daly	**	1945
Korea	*Samuel Streit Coursen*	17342	1949
Korea	*Richard Thomas Shea, Jr.*	18774	1952
Vietnam	*William Atkinson Jones, III*	*14654	1945
Vietnam	*Andre Cavaro Lucas*	19779	1954
Vietnam	Roger Hugh C. Donlon	**	1959
Vietnam	*Frank Stanley Reasoner*	24302	1962
Vietnam	Robert Franklin Foley	24913	1963
Vietnam	Paul William Bucha	25503	1965
Vietnam	*James Alton Gardner*	**	1965

Notes:

Ex - Cadet: **
Army Air Corps or U.S.Air Force: *
Posthumous Award: name is in italics

APPENDIX 2

MULTIPLE DISTINGUISHED SERVICE CROSS RECIPIENTS
(listed by number of DSC awards first, then by AOG #, and then by Class)

CONFLICT	#	NAME	AOG #	CLASS
World War I	3	John Henry Parker	3498	1892
World War I & II	3	Douglas MacArthur	4122	1903
World War I & II	3	William Gaulbert Weaver	5079	1912
World War II	3	James Alward Van Fleet	5404	1915
Moros/ World War I	2	Frank Crandall Bolles	3737	1896
World War I	2	Evan Elias Lewis	4628	1907
World War I & II	2	George Smith Patton, Jr.	4795	1909
World War I & II	2	Robert Lawrence Eichelberger	4817	1909
World War II	2	Harry Albert Flint	5058	1912
World War II/ Korea	2	Walton Harris Walker	5090	1912
World War I	2	Charles Wolcott Ryder	5351	1915
World War I/Siberia	2	Sidney Carroll Graves	5388	1915
World War I & II	2	William Morris Hoge	5505	1916
World War II	2	Matthew Bunker Ridgway	5657	1917(Apr)
World War I & II	2	George Hatton Weems	5695	1917(Apr)
World War II/ Korea	2	Joseph Sladen Bradley	6462	1919
World War II	2	Halstead Clotworthy Fowler	6623	1920
World War II	2	Gordon Byrom Rogers	7345	1924
World War II/ Korea	2	Frank Sayles Bowen, Jr.	7935	1926
World War II	2	John Leonard Hines, Jr.	8038	1927

CONFLICT	#	NAME	AOG #	CLASS
World War II	2	Dudley George Strickler	8187	1927
World War II	2	Robert Tryon Frederick	8349	1928
World War II	2	James Maurice Gavin	8671	1929
World War II/ Korea	2	Louis Victor Hightower	9196	1931
Korea	2	Edwin John Messinger	9197	1931
World War II	2	William Orlando Darby	9762	1933
World War II	2	Reuben Henry Tucker, 3d	10368	1935
World War II	2	Richard Henry Carmichael	* 10551	1936
World War II	2	Creighton Williams Abrams, Jr.	10644	1936
World War II	2	Thomas Edgar Clifford, Jr.	10687	1936
World War II	2	Charles Billingslea	10715	1936
World War II	2	Elery Martin Zehner	10992	1937
Korea	2	James Howard Skeldon	11003	1937
Korea	2	Claire Elwood Hutchin, Jr.	11073	1938
World War II	2	Ralph Burton Praeger	11167	1938
Korea	2	James Henry Lynch	11219	1938
World War II	2	Arthur Fulbrook Gorham	11231	1938
World War II/ Korea	2	John Thomas Corley	11307	1938
Vietnam	2	John Russell Deane, Jr.	12855	1942
World War II	2	William James Higgins	**	1944
Vietnam	2	George Smith Patton	16099	1946
Vietnam	2	Henry Everett Emerson	16460	1947
Korea/Vietnam	2	Ralph Puckett, Jr.	16935	1949
Vietnam	2	Barry Richard McCaffrey	25054	1964

Notes:

Ex - Cadet: **
Army Air Corps: *

APPENDIX 3

DISTINGUISHED SERVICE CROSS RECIPIENTS
(single DSC awards listed by AOG # first, and then by Class)

CONFLICT	NAME	AOG #	CLASS
Indian Campaigns	John A. Kress	**	1862
Indian Campaigns	Charles Braden	2291	1869
Cuba Campaign	Thomas Taylor Knox	2396	1871
Cuba Campaign	James Allen	2438	1872
Philippine Insurrection	James Franklin Bell	2754	1879
Cuba Campaign	Andrew Summers Rowan	2920	1881
World War I	John Bacon McDonald	2930	1881
Cuba Campaign	Charles Henry Muir	3065	1885
World War I	Beaumont Bonaparte Buck	3087	1885
Cuba Campaign	George Logan Byram	3089	1885
World War I	John Joseph Pershing	3126	1886
World War I	Benjamin Andrew Poore	3129	1886
World War I	John Murray Jenkins	3183	1887
World War I	Ulysses Grant McAlexander	3226	1887
Cuba Campaign	Robert Henry Sillman	**	1887
Cuba Campaign	Peyton Conway March	3247	1888
Philippine Insurrection	Charles Dudley Rhodes	3307	1889
World War I	Fred Winchester Sladen	3357	1890

World War I	Edmund Luther Butts	3383	1891
China Relief Exp.	Joseph Frazier	3420	1891
World War I	LaRoy Sunderland Upton	3422	1891
World War I	John Leonard Hines	3432	1891
World War I	Walter Monteith Whitman	3434	1891
World War I	Hanson Edward Ely	3447	1891
Puerto Rico Exp.	Henry Howard Whitney	3460	1892
World War I	Charles Pelot Summerall	3469	1892
World War I	James Haynes Reeves	3471	1892
World War I	Edmund Mortimer Leary	3482	1892
World War I	William David Davis	3505	1892
World War I	Samuel Vinton Ham	3508	1892
Philippine Insurrection	George Hunter McMaster	3509	1892
Cuba Campaign	Hamilton Allen Smith	3559	1894
Philippine Insurrection	Paul Bernard Malone	3579	1894
World War I	George Vidmer	3600	1894
World War I	Harry La Tourrette Cavenaugh	3630	1895
Philippine Insurrection	Perry Lester Miles	3639	1895
Moro Expedition	Charles Bryant Drake	3696	1896
Philippine Insurrection	Edward Leonard King	3717	1896
World War I	Dennis Edward Nolan	3719	1896
World War I	Russell Creamer Langdon	3726	1896
Philippine Insurrection	Claude Hamilton Miller	3764	1897
World War I	Halstead Dorey	3784	1897
World War I	Robert Jayne Maxey	3862	1898
World War I	Robert Halford Peck	3900	1899
Moro Expedition	Henry Leavenworth Harris, Jr	3912	1899
World War I	James Cooper Rhea	3921	1899
World War I	Henry Clay Jewett	4002	1901
World War I	Edmund Loughborough Zane	4104	1901
World War I	William Franklin Harrell	**	1902

World War I	James Andrew Shannon	4158	1903
World War I	George Francis Rozelle, Jr.	4189	1903
World War II	Joseph Warren Stilwell	4246	1904
World War I	Arthur Dryhurst Budd	4300	1904
World War I	Lowe Abeel McClure	4314	1904
World War I	John Buchanan Richardson	4338	1904
World War I	Avery Duane Cummings	4427	1905
World War II	Jonathan Mayhew Wainwright	4477	1906
World War I	Fred Alden Cook	4505	1906
Moro Expedition	Roger Sheffield Parrott	4657	1908
World War I	Edward Seery Hayes	4697	1908
World War II	Simon Bolivar Buckner, Jr.	4699	1908
World War I	Arthur Edward Bouton	4731	1908
World War I	Enoch Barton Garey	4733	1908
World War I	John Harold Muncaster	4738	1908
World War II	Courtney Hicks Hodges	**	1908
World War II	Donald Meredith Beere	4768	1909
World War II	Clifford Bluemel	4845	1909
World War I	Francis Robert Hunter	4847	1909
World War I	Manton Campbell Mitchell	4849	1909
World War I	Creswell Garlington	4854	1910
World War I	Daniel Dee Pullen	4856	1910
World War I	Parker Cromwell Kalloch, Jr.	4894	1910
World War I	Charles Philip Hall	4957	1911
World War II	James Roy Newman Weaver	4987	1911
World War I	Wm. Henry Harrison Morris, Jr.	4991	1911
World War I	Alvan Crosby Sandeford	4998	1911
World War II	John Shirley Wood	5029	1912
World War I	d'Alary Fechet	5039	1912
World War II	Walter Melville Robertson	5059	1912
World War I	Francis Kosier Newcomer	5113	1913

World War I	Brehon Burke Somervell	5211	1914
World War I	Roy Melvin Smyth	5226	1914
World War I	Carl Spaatz	* 5262	1914
World War I	Claude Clarence Paschal	5272	1914
World War II	Orlando Ward	5291	1914
World War II	Ralph Royce	* 5294	1914
World War II	Jens Anderson Doe	5310	1914
World War II	Joseph May Swing	5350	1915
World War I	John William Leonard	5396	1915
World War I	Harry Aloysius Harvey	5423	1915
Korea	George Edward Stratemeyer	* 5459	1915
World War I	John Howard Wills	5477	1916
World War I	William Arthur Snow	5483	1916
World War I	Warner William Carr	5543	1916
World War I	Geoffrey Prescott Baldwin	5549	1916
World War I	Robert Kenneth Whitson	5591	1916
World War I	Paul Gerard Daly	**	1916
World War I	Charles Benjamin Duncan	**	1916
World War I	Harris Jones	5602	1917(Apr)
World War I	John Jefferson Flowers Steiner	5607	1917(Apr)
World War I	William Harrison Saunders	* 5610	1917(Apr)
World War I	James Oscar Green, Jr.	5638	1917(Apr)
World War II	William Kelly Harrison, Jr.	5674	1917(Apr)
World War II	Ernest Nason Harmon	5677	1917(Apr)
World War I	Godfrey Neil Wyke	**	1917(Apr)
World War II	Norman Daniel Cota	5680	1917(Apr)
World War II	Mark Wayne Clark	5711	1917
World War II	Harris Marcy Melasky	5722	1917
World War I	Charles Dashiel Harris	5745	1917(Aug)
World War I	John Thornton Knight, Jr.	5770	1917(Aug)
World War I	Henry Anson Barber, Jr.	5771	1917(Aug)

World War I	John Henry Norton	5829	1917(Aug)
World War I	Kenneth Paul Murray	5841	1917(Aug)
World War I	Roger Walton Stembridge	5842	1917(Aug)
World War I	Leo Vincent Warner	5846	1917(Aug)
World War I	Onslow Sherburne Rolfe	5849	1917(Aug)
World War I	Harry Cooper Barnes, Jr.	5862	1917(Aug)
World War I	Josephus Benjamin Wilson	5870	1917(Aug)
World War I	Frank Sidney Long	5883	1917(Aug)
World War I	Horace Harding	5888	1917(Aug)
World War I	Ewing M. Taylor	**	1917(Aug)
World War II	Hugh John Casey	5894	1918
World War II	Eugene Mead Caffey	5929	1918
World War II	George Bittman Barth	6006	1918
World War II	Harry Benham Sherman	6008	1918
World War II	Frederic Bates Butler	6036	1918(Nov)
Siberia	Paul Wilkins Kendall	6212	1918(Nov)
World War II	Jesse Lewis Gibney	6231	1918(Nov)
World War II	Anthony Clement McAuliffe	6284	1919
World War II	James Holden Phillips	6355	1919
World War II	Willard Gordon Wyman	6383	1919
World War II	Irvin Alexander	6462	1919
World War II	Wayne Cliffton Zimmerman	6470	1919
World War II	John David Frederick	6489	1919
World War II	Verne Donald Mudge	6615	1920
World War II	Henry Chester Hine, Jr.	6676	1920
World War II	Clovis Ethelbert Byers	6707	1920
World War II	Maxwell Davenport Taylor	6831	1922
World War II	Charles Hancock Reed	6881	1922
World War II	James Edward Rees	6911	1922
World War II	William Henry Schildroth	6920	1922
World War II	James Clyde Fry	6958	1922

World War II	David Larr	7013	1923
World War II	Howard Edward C. Breitung	7158	1923
Korea	Henry Granville Fisher	7201	1923
World War II	Hal Clark Granberry	7202	1923
Korea	Earle Everard Partridge	* 7226	1924
World War II	Charles Trueman Lanham	7293	1924
Korea	Richard Warburton Stephens	7294	1924
World War II	Uzal Girard Ent	* 7329	1924
World War II	Samuel Glenn Conley	7433	1924
World War II	William Olmstead Eareckson	* 7504	1924
World War II	Francis Robert Stevens	* 7508	1924
World War II	George Winfered Smythe	7545	1924
World War II	Bruce Cooper Clarke	7658	1925
World War II	Aubrey Strode Newman	7690	1925
World War II	Welborn Barton Griffith, Jr.	7785	1925
Korea	Marcel Gustave Crombez	7789	1925
Korea	Wayne Carleton Smith	7799	1925
World War II	John Llewellyn Lewis	7814	1925
Korea	George Bateman Peploe	7838	1925
World War II	Russell Potter Reeder, Jr.	7995	1926
World War II	Charles Draper William Canham	7997	1926
World War II	Thomas John Hall Trapnell	8071	1927
World War II	Leander LaChance Doan	8128	1927
World War II	Joseph Ganahl	8143	1927
World War II	Carl Elliott Lundquist	8178	1927
Korea	Guy Stanley Meloy, Jr.	8181	1927
World War II	Raymond Earle Bell	8186	1927
World War II	Philip DeWitt Ginder	8193	1927
World War II	Martin Moses	8213	1927
World War II	Nathan Bedford Forrest	* 8277	1928
World War II	Russell Alger Wilson	* 8317	1928

World War II	David Raymond Gibbs	* 8318	1928
World War II	Frederick Lewis Anderson	* 8328	1928
World War II	John Southworth Upham, Jr.	8331	1928
World War II	Robert Falligant Travis	* 8340	1928
Korea	William Henry Tunner	* 8348	1928
World War II	Ralph Edward Koon	* 8350	1928
World War II	Lionel Charles McGarr	8378	1928
World War II	Roger Maxwell Ramey	* 8385	1928
World War II	George Ferrow Smith	* 8412	1928
Korea	Emmett O'Donnell, Jr.	* 8453	1928
World War II	Paul Williams Thompson	8499	1929
Korea	Paul Lamar Freeman, Jr.	8699	1929
World War II	William Lester Nave	8732	1929
World War II	Arthur Knight Noble	8775	1929
World War II	Frederick Walker Castle	* 8792	1929
World War II	Irvin Rudolph Schimmelpfennig	8810	1930
World War II	Walter Campbell Sweeney, Jr.	* 8845	1930
World War II	Alva Revista Fitch	8879	1930
World War II	Sidney Clay Wooten	8892	1930
World War II	Raymond Davis Millener	8906	1930
World War II	George Wareham Gibbs	8944	1930
World War II	James Sawyer Luckett	8976	1930
Korea	Ned Dalton Moore	8979	1930
World War II	Christian Hudgins Clarke	8980	1930
Korea	Allan Duard MacLean	8998	1930
World War II	Francis Hill Dohs	9002	1930
Korea	Miller Osborne Perry	9120	1931
Korea	William Harris Isbell, Jr.	9167	1931
World War II	John Knight Waters	9175	1931
World War II	Jacob Edward Smart	* 9210	1931
Korea	Richard Francis Reidy	9251	1931

World War II	John Hubert Mathews	9320	1931
World War II	Loren Boyd Hillsinger	* 9396	1932
World War II	William Massello, Jr.	9419	1932
World War II	Stephen Michael Mellnik	9424	1932
World War II	William Halford Maguire	9488	1932
World War II	John Clinton Welborn	9535	1932
World War II	John Garnett Coughlin	9570	1932
World War II	Robert Lee Scott, Jr.	* 9580	1932
Korea	William Allen Harris	9605	1933
World War II	James Leo Dalton, 2d	9729	1933
World War II	Edgar Collins Doleman	9760	1933
World War II	Raymond Emerson Kendall	9772	1933
World War II	Harold Keith Johnson	9817	1933
World War II	Joseph Brice Crawford	9845	1933
World War II	Lawrence Kermit White	9872	1933
World War II	Paul Douglas Wood	9926	1933
World War II	John Baird Shinberger	9930	1933
World War II	Russell William Volckmann	10121	1934
Korea	John Lathrop Throckmorton	10205	1935
World War II	Elmer John Koehler	10225	1935
World War II	James Frank Skells	10303	1935
Korea	Joseph Rieber Russ	10333	1935
World War II	Autrey Joseph Maroun	10338	1935
World War II	George Frederick Marshall	10341	1935
World War II	Henry Thomas Cherry, Jr.	10362	1935
World War II	Wilson Dudley Coleman	10388	1935
World War II	Robert Eugene Tucker	10412	1935
World War II	George Madison Jones	10439	1935
World War II	John Edward Kelly	10504	1936
World War II	Clinton Utterback True	* 10619	1936
Korea	John Harold Daly	10632	1936

World War II	John Henry Chiles	10643	1936
Korea	John Hersey Michaelis	10676	1936
World War II	Henry Andrews Mucci	10723	1936
World War II	James Nixon Peale, Jr.	10854	1937
World War II	Edward C. David Scherrer	10860	1937
World War II	Floyd Joaquin Pell	* 10871	1937
World War II	Edward Marion Postlethwait	10888	1937
World War II	Charles Robert Meyer	10934	1937
World War II	Charles Andrews Sprague	* 10941	1937
World War II	Robert Besson	10943	1937
World War II	William Grover Hipps	* 10959	1937
World War II	Delk McCorkle Oden	10977	1937
World War II	Colin Purdie Kelly, Jr.	* 10983	1937
Vietnam	John Jarvis Tolson, 3rd	10998	1937
World War II	James Francis Faber	11001	1937
World War II	Morton David Magoffin	* 11019	1937
World War II	James Theo Posey	* 11022	1937
World War II	Robert Claude McCabe	11070	1938
World War II	Barry Duran Browne	11080	1938
World War II	Richard Gay Ivey	11097	1938
World War II	John Harland Swenson	11125	1938
World War II	Joseph Rhett Barker, II	11137	1938
World War II	Charles Loyd Jackson	11189	1938
World War II	Gordon Madison Clarkson	11204	1938
World War II	David Owen Byars, Jr.	11255	1938
World War II	Ben Sternberg	11268	1938
World War II	Charles Joseph Denholm	11275	1938
World War II	Arthur Anthony Maloney	11279	1938
World War II	Robert Howard York	11323	1938
World War II	Andrew Jackson Goodpaster	11336	1939
World War II	Julian Johnson Ewell	11388	1939

World War II	Haskett Lynch Conner, Jr.	11452	1939
World War II	Elbert Owen Meals	* 11470	1939
World War II	Paul Vernon Tuttle, Jr.	11495	1939
World War II	Raymond Bradner Marlin	11498	1939
World War II	John George Pickard	* 11515	1939
World War II	William Joseph Boyle	11555	1939
Korea	Welborn Griffin Dolvin	11582	1939
World War II	Walter Martin Higgins, Jr.	11589	1939
World War II	Harry Wm. Osborne Kinnard, Jr.	11592	1939
World War II	Robert Watson Crandall	11612	1939
World War II	Rudyard Kipling Grimes	11633	1939
World War II	Edwin Joseph Ostberg	11645	1939
World War II	William LeRoy Turner	11656	1939
World War II	Robert Beirne Spragins	11683	1939
World War II	Bernard George Teeters	11684	1939
World War II	Stanley Robert Larsen	11698	1939
World War II	Richard Van Wyck Negley, Jr.	* 11712	1939
Korea	Charles Bradford Smith	11717	1939
World War II	George Thomas Coleman	11754	1939
World War II	Edward Smith Hamilton	11769	1939
World War II	James Walter Wilson	* 11778	1939
World War II	Lindsay Coates Herkness, Jr.	11785	1939
World War II	Charles Thompson Horner, Jr.	**	1939
World War II	Herbert Edward Pace, Jr.	11817	1940
World War II	Donald Haldeman Baumer	11893	1940
World War II	Donald Vivian Bennett	11907	1940
World War II	Michael Paulick	11966	1940
World War II	William Edward Buck, Jr.	* 11978	1940
World War II	Alan Martin Strock	12005	1940
World War II	John Herold Wohner	12049	1940
World War II	Bryce Frederic Denno	12068	1940

World War II	Wallace Leo Clement	12074	1940
World War II	Leland George Cagwin	12107	1940
World War II	Louis Gonzaga Mendez, Jr.	12169	1940
World War II	Sidney Vincent Bingham, Jr.	12176	1940
World War II	William Francis Coleman	* 12187	1940
World War II	Julian Aaron Cook	12197	1940
World War II	William Powell Litton	* 12207	1940
World War II	Theodore Ross Milton	* 12214	1940
World War II	Wadsworth Paul Clapp	12242	1941
World War II	John Adams Brooks, III	* 12385	1941
World War II	William Graham Gillis, Jr.	12468	1941
World War II	Ira Boswell Cheaney, Jr.	12524	1941
World War II	George Scratchley Brown	* 12581	1941
World War II	James Lawrence Kaiser	12647	1941
Korea	William Thomas McDaniel	12650	1941
World War II	Thomas Francis Farrell, Jr.	12732	1942
World War II	Alexander McCarrell Patch, III	12743	1942
World War II	Wayne Norbury Bolefahr	* 12928	1942
World War II	James Simmons Timothy	13013	1942
World War II	Louis Theodore Seith	* 13062	1943(Jan)
World War II	James Berhardt Cobb	* 13121	1943(Jan)
World War II	Lawrence Philip Bischoff, Jr.	13178	1943(Jan)
World War II	George Mayer Eberle	13251	1943(Jan)
World War II	Charles Alvin Wirt	13335	1943(Jan)
World War II	William Johnston Hovde	* 13363	1943(Jan)
World War II	Carlos Maurice Talbott	* 13407	1943(Jan)
Vietnam	Bernard William Rogers	13459	1943
World War II	John Price Mattfeldt	13543	1943
World War II	Donald Charles Pence	13565	1943
World War II	Paul Gregory Atkinson	* 13567	1943
Korea	Harold Halsey Dunwoody	13793	1943

Korea	John Henry Nelson	13917	1943
World War II	Edward Charles Christl, Jr.	14082	1944
Korea	Claude Kitchin Josey	14825	1945
Korea	William Doran Clark	14840	1945
Korea	John Joseph Powers, Jr.	14870	1945
Korea	Smith Barton Chamberlain	14983	1945
Vietnam	Harold Gregory Moore, Jr.	15076	1945
Korea	Andrew John Gatsis	15286	1945
World War II	William Middleton Grimes, Jr.	**	1945
Korea	John Gillespie Hill, Jr.	15392	1946
Korea	James Von Kanel Ladd	15873	1946
Korea	Charles Alexander FitzGerald	16005	1946
Vietnam	Stephen Eugene Gray	16097	1946
Korea	Charles Leroy Wesolowsky	16119	1946
Vietnam	Alexander Meigs Haig, Jr.	16375	1947
Korea	Henry Tomlinson MacGill	16395	1947
Korea	Edward Ansel White	16550	1948
Korea	James Cornelius Ruddell, Jr	16575	1948
Vietnam	John Winn McEnery	16582	1948
Korea	Alfred Julius Anderson	17185	1949
Korea	William Hale Wilbur, Jr.	17220	1949
Korea	Courtenay Chirm Davis, Jr.	17307	1949
Korea	Wilfred Donald Miller	17567	1950
Korea	Peter Howland Monfore	17651	1950
Korea	Joseph Ross Franklin	17656	1950
Korea	George Ervine Hannan	17685	1950
Korea	Charles Lewis Butler	17764	1950
Korea	John Michael Murphy	17802	1950
Korea	James Cross Barnes, Jr.	17933	1950
Korea	Charles Kohl Farabaugh	17944	1950
Korea	David Ralph Hughes	17958	1950

Korea	Mark James Hanna	18002	1950
Korea	Frank Riley Loyd, Jr.	18013	1950
Korea	Joseph Gordon Clemons, Jr.	18024	1951
Korea	John Allen Hemphill	18229	1951
Korea	Richard Rogier McCullough	18384	1951
Korea	George Massie Gividen, Jr.	18417	1951
Korea	George Peter Psihas	18455	1951
Vietnam	Robert Silber McGowan	18682	1952
Vietnam	Glen Kay Otis	19074	1953
Vietnam	Guy Stanley Meloy, III	19361	1953
Vietnam	Louis Carson Wagner, Jr.	19614	1954
Vietnam (AFC)	William Davis Burroughs	* 20184	1955
Vietnam	Thomas Weller McCarthy	20351	1955
Vietnam	William Clifford Maus, Jr.	20419	1955
Vietnam	John Carl Johnson	20899	1956
Vietnam	John Charles Bahnsen, Jr.	21039	1956
Vietnam	William Purnell Baxter	21076	1956
Vietnam	Leon Delbert Bieri	21245	1957
Vietnam	Morris Ralph McBride	21252	1957
Vietnam	Thomas Henry Harvey, Jr.	22182	1958
Vietnam	Raymond Forrest R. Tomlinson	22203	1958
Vietnam	William Joseph Mullen, III	22433	1959
Vietnam	Gilbert Noyes Dorland	22691	1959
Vietnam	Charles Edward Getz	22709	1959
Vietnam	William Stanley Carpenter, Jr.	22922	1960
Vietnam	James Armitt Scott, III	23529	1961
Vietnam	Patrick Mickael Trinkle	23568	1961
Vietnam	James Michael Coyle	23594	1961
Vietnam	Allan Raymond Wetzel	23633	1961
Vietnam	John Phillips Lawton	**	1961
Vietnam (NC)	Marshall Nichols Carter	24005	1962

Vietnam	Timothy James Grogan	24610	1963
Vietnam	Luther Lee Woods	24623	1963
Vietnam	Malcolm Dean Otis	24775	1963
Vietnam (NC)	John Raymond Ahern	24785	1963
Vietnam	Louis Albert Mari	24909	1963
Vietnam	Robert Dean Stowell	25712	1965
Vietnam	Claude Keyes Hudson	25843	1965
Vietnam	John Hulsey Hays	25858	1965
Vietnam	James Harry Hall	* 25910	1965
Vietnam	Ronald James Riley	26028	1965
Vietnam	Gerald Thomas Cecil	26469	1966
Vietnam	Robert Michael Snell	26500	1966
Vietnam	Robert Lawrence Fergusson	**	1966
Vietnam	Gary William Carlson	27088	1967
Vietnam	William Whitaker Horn	27152	1967
Vietnam	Raymond James Enners	27213	1967
Vietnam	William James Peplinski	27436	1968
Vietnam	John Oscar Benson	27571	1968
Vietnam	William Francis Little, III	27738	1968
Vietnam	Ross Stanley Kelly	29405	1970

Notes:

Ex - Cadet: **
Army Air Corps or U.S. Air Force Officer: *
Air Force Cross awarded to an Air Force Officer: AFC
Navy Cross awarded to a Marine Corps Officer: NC